What Is Coronavirus?

How It Infects, How It Spreads, and How to Stay Safe

Written and illustrated by
Sabbithry Persad, MBA

Edited by
Camilly P. Pires de Mello, PhD
and
Viveca Giongo, PhD

FIREWATER
MEDIA GROUP

Contents

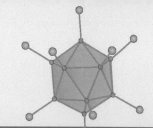

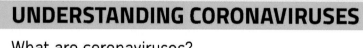

CORONAVIRUS AND THE ENVIRONMENT

COMBATTING CORONAVIRUS

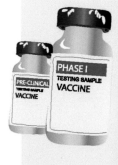

EXTRAS

VIRUS BASICS

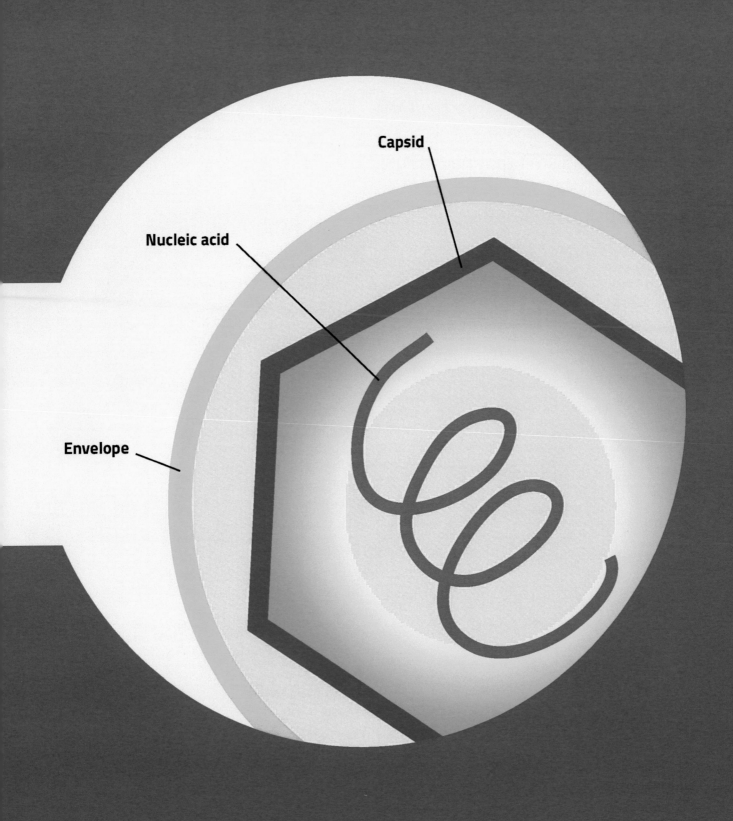

What are viruses?

People talk a lot about viruses, but what are they? Viruses are one of the four major types of germs: bacteria, viruses, fungi, and protozoa. Viruses are microscopic organisms that have four main characteristics: structure, size, shape, and host dependency.

Nucleic acid

The nucleic acid core contains the nucleic acid (genetic material, DNA or RNA)—the main information-carrying molecules found in all living organisms and viruses.

Capsid

The nucleic acid is enclosed by a protein coat called the capsid, which protects the genetic material. The capsid contains protein subunits called capsomers.

Virus Structure

There are many different viruses, but all of them have a few things in common: the nucleic acid core, capsid, and envelope.

Envelope

Some viruses have an extra outer envelope to protect the capsid. The protective envelope surface forms from parts of the host cell's cytoplasmic membrane.

Virus Shape

Virus shapes vary widely and are formed by arrangement of capsomeres. Some arrangements look like tall spiders. Others look like spiky porcupines. The most common arrangements are: helical, icosahedral, and complex.

Parvovirus
23-26 nm

Dengue virus
46-60 nm

Virus Size

Viruses are a thousand times smaller than bacteria. They come in a variety of sizes ranging from about 5 to 300 nanometers (nm) in diameter. More recently, scientists have identified larger viruses like Mimiviruses (2003) and Pandoraviruses (2013), which have an average diameter of 0.5 micrometers (μm) and Tupanviruses (2018), which have an average length of ~1.2 micrometers (μm).

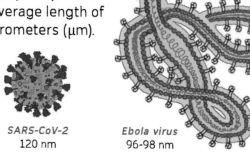

Rabies lyssavirus
180 x 80 nm

HIV
120 nm

SARS-CoV-2
120 nm

Ebola virus
96-98 nm

0 nm   200 nm   400 nm   600 nm

Scale

Bird host
(Duck adenovirus)

Bird host
(Chicken anemia virus)

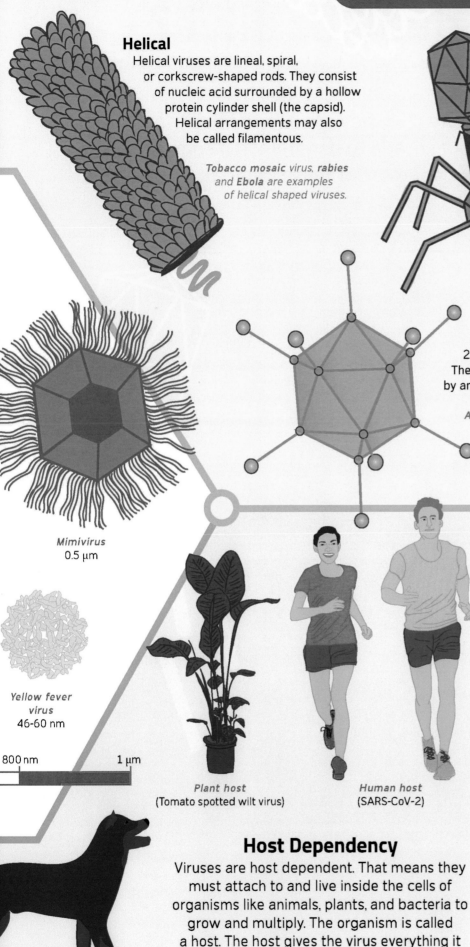

Helical

Helical viruses are lineal, spiral, or corkscrew-shaped rods. They consist of nucleic acid surrounded by a hollow protein cylinder shell (the capsid). Helical arrangements may also be called filamentous.

*Tobacco mosaic virus, **rabies** and **Ebola** are examples of helical shaped viruses.*

Complex

Complex viruses are like a hybrid between helical and icosahedral forms. They are pleomorphic (having two or more forms), irregularly shaped, or have complex structures. They consist of the nucleic acid inside the icosahedral shape and the special function helical tail.

***T4 bacteriophage** is an example of a complex shaped virus.*

Icosahedral

Icosahedral viruses may also be called spherical because they are formed by 20 triangular faces and 12 corners. They consist of a nucleic acid surrounded by an icosahedral (20-sided) capsid.

*Adenovirus, **herpes**, and **polio** are examples of icosahedral shaped viruses.*

Mimivirus
0.5 µm

Yellow fever virus
46-60 nm

800 nm   1 µm

Plant host
(Tomato spotted wilt virus)

Human host
(SARS-CoV-2)

Canine host
(Canine distemper virus)

Host Dependency

Viruses are host dependent. That means they must attach to and live inside the cells of organisms like animals, plants, and bacteria to grow and multiply. The organism is called a host. The host gives the virus everything it needs to make more virus. Outside a host, viruses may not survive for very long.

Fast Facts

RNA is an abbreviation. It stands for ribonucleic acid.

Approximately 1 billion viruses can live on the end of one eyelash!

There are 10,000,000 nanometers in one centimeter, which is about as wide as a fingernail!

The smallest known viruses are circoviruses, which are 20 nanometers in diameter.

Viruses are very small and most of them can be seen only by TEM (transmission electron microscopy).

The term "virus" is Latin for poison.

Are viruses dead or alive?

Viruses challenge the concept of a clear distinction between living and dead. Scientists are not sure if viruses are living or nonliving. Biologists use a common set of criteria to understand if something is alive or not. Viruses do not meet most of these criteria.

Biologists ask these questions when determining if something is living:

Does it use energy?
Living things use energy. They must get food to fuel the cell's activity. Animals eat other animals for energy. Plants captures the Sun's energy to make their own food.

Viruses, on the other hand, are not cells. When outside a host cell, viruses have no activity inside them, and have no need for food. When a virus is inside a host cell, the host cell needs energy to make more virus.

Does it respond to the environment?
Living things react to their environment. They have a way of sensing the world around them and can respond to changes.

Viruses cannot move by themselves. Viruses can react to some changes in their environment through evolution of their genetic material. They adapt through genetic mutations caused by rapid virus production.

Does it grow, develop, and die?
Living things grow or get bigger.

Viruses do nothing inside their protein coat, therefore they do not grow.

Does it divide or reproduce by itself?
Living things reproduce by themselves. Cells have everything they need to reproduce and make copies of their genetic material (DNA).

Viruses have genetic material (DNA or RNA), too, but they do not have the parts to copy their genetic material themselves. Instead, viruses infect cells and use the cells' machinery to copy their genetic material in order to make more virus.

Does it have cells?
Living things have cells.

Viruses are not single-celled organisms. They do not have cells, a cell membrane, or other organelles that cells have. They are a little more than a strand of genetic material (DNA or RNA) protected by a protein coating.

Envelope (E) protein (some viruses)

Spike (S) protein

A: Since viruses do not meet most of the criteria considered to be a living thing, they are not considered living creatures. They are nonliving particles with some chemical characteristics similar to those of life.

But, the jury is still out. Recently, scientist found a new virus called Mimivirus that contains the parts to make a copy of its DNA and contains numerous genes that we thought exist only in cellular organisms. This changes the understanding and places viruses in a "questionable" zone, because Mimivirus meets more of the living criteria.

Virus anatomy

A virus is an infectious agent made up of nucleic acid (DNA or RNA) wrapped in a protein coat called a capsid. Viruses have no nucleus, no organelles, no cytoplasm or cell membrane—they are non-cellular.

Nucleocapsid (N) protein

Capsid (protein coat)

Nucleic acid (genetic material, DNA or RNA)

Cell anatomy

A cell is the basic building block of all known living organisms. It is the smallest unit capable of independent reproduction. A cell is made of proteins, lipids, carbohydrates, and nucleic acid surrounded by a cell membrane. Some organisms are made up of one cell, while others are made up of trillions of cells.

Nucleus

Ribosomes

Cytoplasm

Endoplasmic reticulum

Golgi apparatus

Cell membrane

Can Viruses Be Killed?

Most scientists believe that viruses cannot be killed. They can only be inactivated. Once inactive, infection is unlikely.

Soap

If a virus is outside the host and has an envelope lipid shell, it can be inactivated with common soap. The soap breaks apart the lipid shell to inactivate the virus.

Examples of enveloped viruses are SARS-CoV-2, influenza, and human immunodeficiency virus (HIV).

Wash away with disinfectants

ETHYL ALCOHOL

If a virus is outside the host and is non-enveloped, soap does not inactivate it. Instead, disinfectants such as alcohol or bleach (active ingredient sodium hypochlorite) can disrupt the virus's structure and inactivate it.

Examples of non-enveloped viruses are rhinoviruses and adenoviruses that cause the common cold.

!

Disinfectants can irritate the mucous membrane, skin, and airways, as well as react with other chemicals.

Medicines

If viruses are inside their host, medicines such as antiviral drugs block their replication.

Immune system

When no treatment is available, only a person's immune system can defeat viruses.

Fast Facts

Human beings are made up of more than 75 trillion cells!

●

DNA (genetic material) is referred to as the "code for life." Having DNA is an important step toward being classified as alive. DNA controls the evolution of the cell and the organism. But unlike cells, viruses cannot use their genetic material by themselves.

●

Viruses have no legs and cannot move on their own.

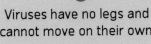
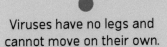

9

How viruses infect and multiply

When a virus infects a cell, it injects its genetic material (DNA or RNA) inside the cell and uses the cell's machinery to create more viruses. The newly formed virus particles, called virions, then leave the host cell and infect nearby cells.

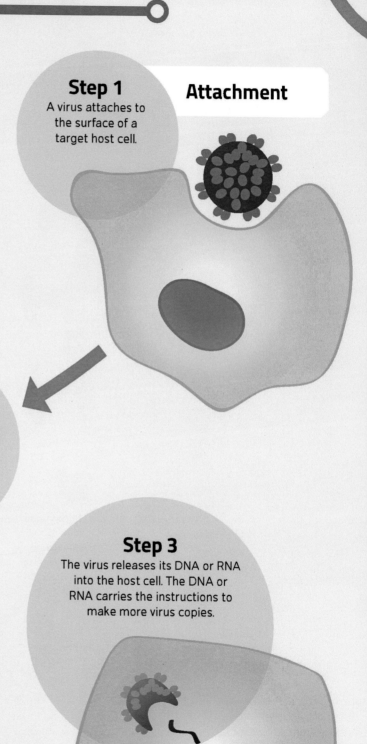

Step 1
A virus attaches to the surface of a target host cell.

Attachment

Entry

Step 2
The host cell engulfs the virus by endocytosis and fusion.

Step 3
The virus releases its DNA or RNA into the host cell. The DNA or RNA carries the instructions to make more virus copies.

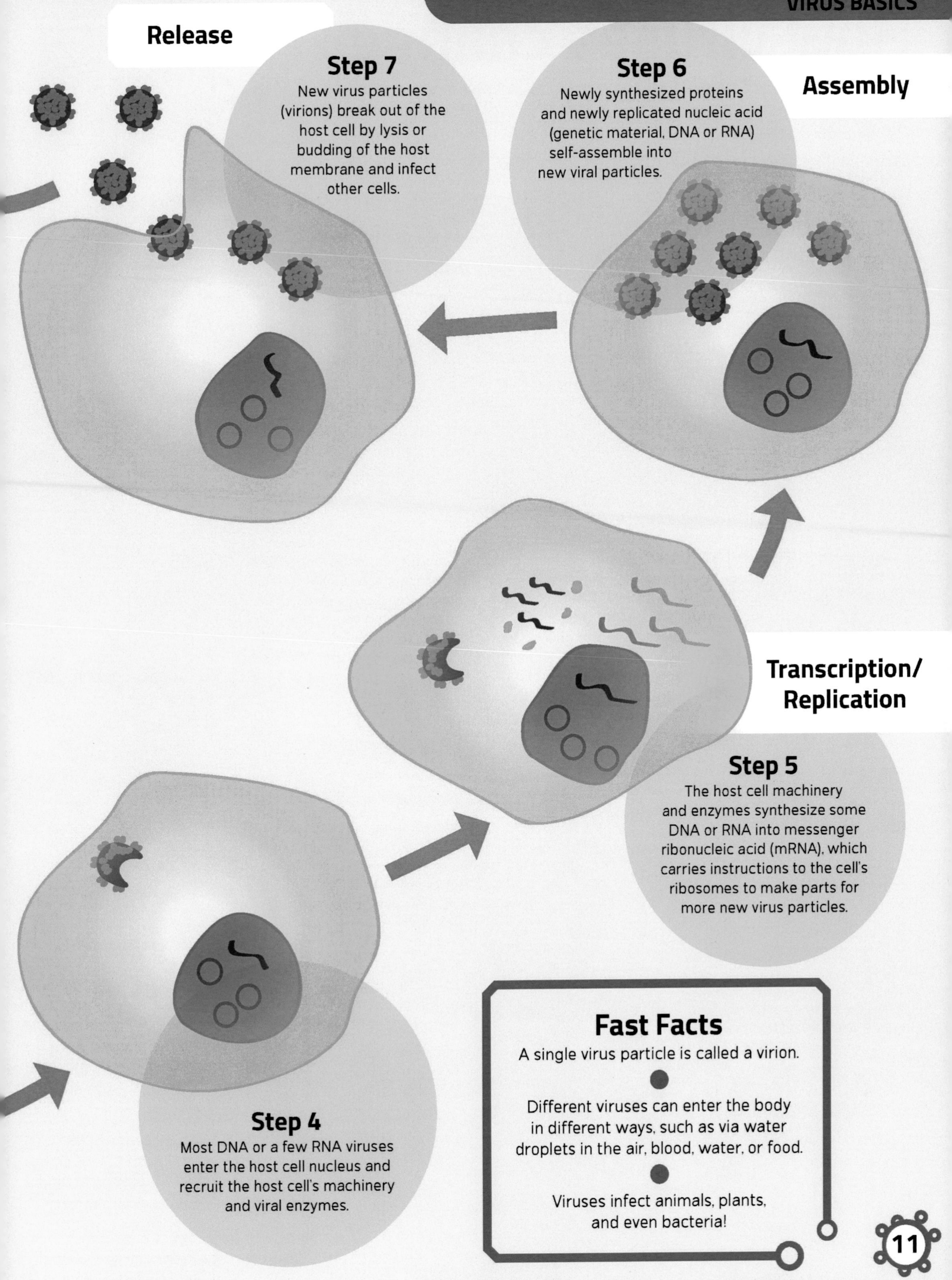

Release

Step 7
New virus particles (virions) break out of the host cell by lysis or budding of the host membrane and infect other cells.

Step 6
Newly synthesized proteins and newly replicated nucleic acid (genetic material, DNA or RNA) self-assemble into new viral particles.

Assembly

**Transcription/
Replication**

Step 5
The host cell machinery and enzymes synthesize some DNA or RNA into messenger ribonucleic acid (mRNA), which carries instructions to the cell's ribosomes to make parts for more new virus particles.

Step 4
Most DNA or a few RNA viruses enter the host cell nucleus and recruit the host cell's machinery and viral enzymes.

Fast Facts
A single virus particle is called a virion.

●

Different viruses can enter the body in different ways, such as via water droplets in the air, blood, water, or food.

●

Viruses infect animals, plants, and even bacteria!

How viruses change

As viruses spread, they constantly adapt to their environment. This is a normal process of evolution referred to as "antigenic variation." Antigenic variation could also alter the proteins on the virus's surface. This allows the virus to avoid the host's immune response.

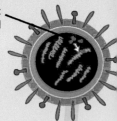

RNA genetic material

RNA has gradual minor changes

Antigenic Drift (Slow Minor Genetic Change)

During virus replication, sometimes there are gradual minor changes that modify the virus's genetic code. These random deviations or errors are called mutations. When the virus is not able to correct the small accidental errors, each new generation of virus will be slightly different. The frequent and natural mutation differences build up over time and form new virus strains--new genetic variants or subtypes. This slow genetic change is called antigenic drift.

RNA has gradual minor changes

Antigenic Drift and Influenza

The influenza virus uses two proteins to get in and out of a human cell. These proteins live on the virus's surface and are called hemagglutinin (HA) and neuraminidase (NA).

If you were previously infected with the influenza virus, and you got reinfected, your body would recognize these proteins (antigens—foreign substances) and your immune system would produce antibodies to block the virus from infecting cells.

RNA has gradual minor changes

Antibodies latch onto the virus protein and prevent the virus from attaching itself to cells.

If, however, genetic mutations accrued and "drifted" enough to form a new strain, your body would not recognize the HA and NA proteins, making you vulnerable to infection.

Hemagglutinin (HA)

Neuraminidase (NA)

Antibodies unable to latch onto the virus because the virus's protein shape has changed. The immune system now needs to create new antibodies with the right shape to latch onto the virus's new protein shape.

RNA has accrued mutations, forming a new virus strain

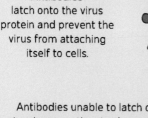

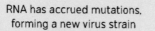

Fast Facts

Viruses have the greatest biodiversity on the planet. There are more viruses in a liter of coastal seawater than people on earth!

DNA virus mutations are approximate to those of eukaryotic cells. And, RNA viruses have much higher mutation rates than DNA viruses

Antigenic Shift
(Sudden Major Genetic Change)

In contrast to drift, antigenic shift occurs less frequently. It is an abrupt, major change that exchanges part of the genetic material (whole or fragments) between related or unrelated viruses that enable a virus strain to jump from one animal species to another. The shift can happen by genetic recombination (homologous or nonhomologous) or reassortment.

1

Nonhomologous recombination (with host or other organism)

The natural recombining of **gene fragments** from one virus and an unrelated virus strain or organism cell coinfect the same host cell and create a new virus strain.

Gene fragments from a virus in a host, such as a chicken, recombines with unrelated viral or cellular gene fragments from the same host to create a new virus strain. This hybrid can overcome natural barriers and "spillover" from one species to another.

2

Homologous recombination

The natural recombining of **gene fragments** from two related viruses of different parent strains coinfect the same host cell and create a new virus strain.

Two related virus strains from one animal, such as a chicken, coinfect the same cell in that chicken. The gene fragments mix and mutate in the chicken, creating a completely new subtype that can spread to another animal it has not yet infected, such as a duck, pig, or human.

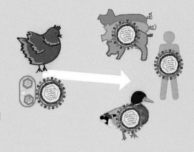

3

Reassortment

The natural replacement of **whole genes** from two or more different virus strains.

A virus from one animal, such as a chicken, infects another animal, such as a duck. The same duck also gets infected by another virus from another animal, such as a pig. The two viruses coinfect a single cell, then mix and mutate in the duck, creating a completely new subtype strain that can then spread to humans.

All virus strains are variants, but not all variants are strains.

Strain vs. Mutation vs. Variant

The term strain is used when referring to a virus because a virus is a strain of a wider virus family. When a virus mutates with significant changes to the biology of the way a virus behaves, the change is referred to as a variant.

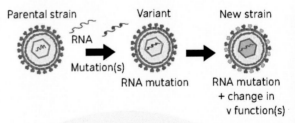

Parental strain — RNA Mutation(s) → Variant — RNA mutation → New strain — RNA mutation + change in v function(s)

Antigenic Shift and Pandemics

Antigenic shift is associated with pandemics. If a new virus strain causes illness and can be transmitted easily from person to person, the virus may cause an epidemic or pandemic strain. Pandemic viruses occur when proteins are not mutated, but are replaced by completely different proteins combined from different strains. Because the virus has new proteins, people do not have pre-existing antibody protection.

Antigenic Shift and Influenza

The 1957 influenza A (H2N2) and 1968 influenza A (H3N2) human pandemics were formed from avian and human viruses. The 2009 influenza A (H1N1) human pandemic started in birds, then moved to humans, and finally moved on to pigs. In all those instances, the new strain was unfamiliar to the hosts' immune systems, and, because the strain was unfamiliar, it caused greater illness.

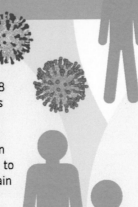

Genomic Sequencing

SARS-CoV-2 is constantly changing, leading to new variants over time. Scientists use a process called genomic sequencing to decode the virus's genetic information. They analyze a virus sample taken from an infected person and compare it with other cases. Genomic sequencing allows scientists to track the virus and understand how it changes over time. As the virus is transmitted to more and more people, differences between variants become more apparent over time.

How viruses jump from animals to humans

When people disturb the natural wildlife habitat, destroy their homes, or even eat them, viruses and other pathogens, diseases, and infections can naturally move from vertebrate animals to humans. This process is called zoonosis.

Zoonosis

Zoonosis has many ways of transmission.

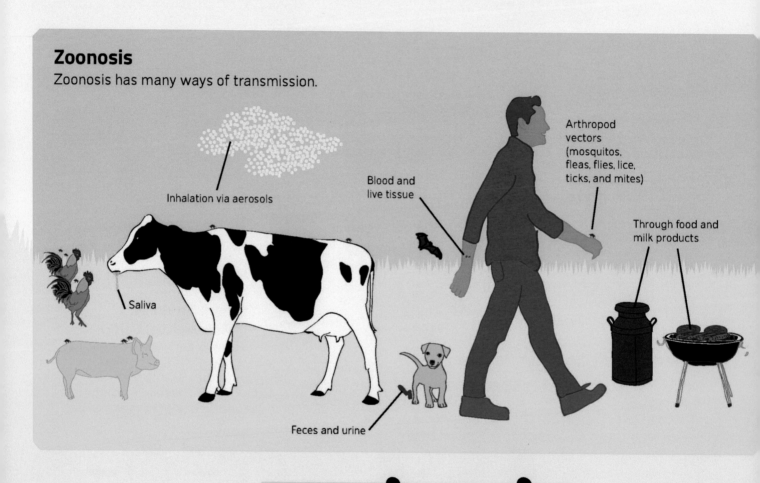

Inhalation via aerosols

Blood and live tissue

Arthropod vectors (mosquitos, fleas, flies, lice, ticks, and mites)

Through food and milk products

Saliva

Feces and urine

Possible SARS-CoV-2 Zoonotic Disease Transmission Paths

Infected human infects another human.

Infected bat infects another animal.

Infected animal *intermediate* host or vector infects human (spillover event).

Virus Detective Tools

Scientists look for clues in the virus's genetic material to learn about its ancestry. They know that a virus multiplies and sometimes mutates in that process. Some mutations hurt and damage the virus, while some help it to thrive.

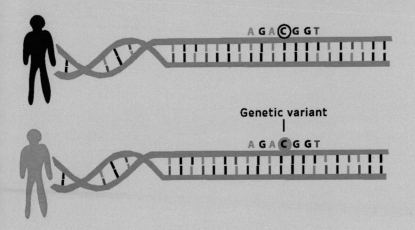

Genetic variant

Investigating
SARS-CoV-2 Zoonotic Origin

Mutations that thrive have a signature that connects one mutation to previous mutations. This signature allows scientists to work backward. They sketch a family tree to find a common ancestor. Similarly, zooming into the genetic material shows a detailed blueprint of the virus's activities. When the signature and blueprint are placed side-by-side and compared letter-by-letter, scientists can see if they match.

Fast Facts

6 out of every 10 infectious diseases in humans are spread from animals.

3 out of 4 new or emerging infectious diseases come from animals.

It is estimated that zoonoses are responsible for 2.5 billion cases of human illness and 2.7 million human deaths worldwide each year.

Zooanthroponosis or "reverse zoonosis" is an infection transmitted from humans to animals.

Viruses may undergo adaptive evolution in the animal host, which could enhance transmission.

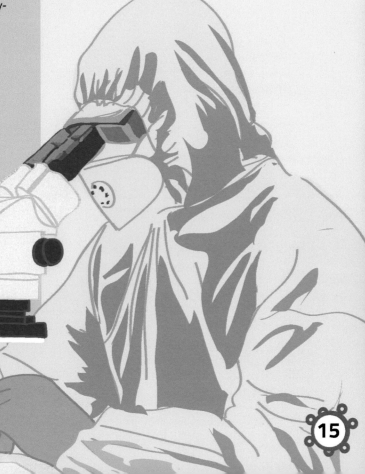

Viruses and diseases

Some viruses cause viral diseases in humans and other animals. What is a viral disease? It's an illness or sickness with specific symptoms. You may have already had a common type of viral disease called the common cold or the flu.

Seasonal Viral Diseases

When a viral disease like the flu returns year after year, it is referred to as seasonal. At least 68 viral diseases are seasonal.

Why does the flu keep returning? When the influenza virus that causes the flu slowly mutates, newer strains emerge. When flu season returns, strains from previous years have slowly drifted. Newer strains become dominant, making the previous years' vaccine ineffective. Researchers must develop a brand-new vaccine for newer strains.

A calendar year will see outbreaks of flu in the winter, chickenpox in the spring, and polio in the summer. Flu season happens annually, typically between February and December.

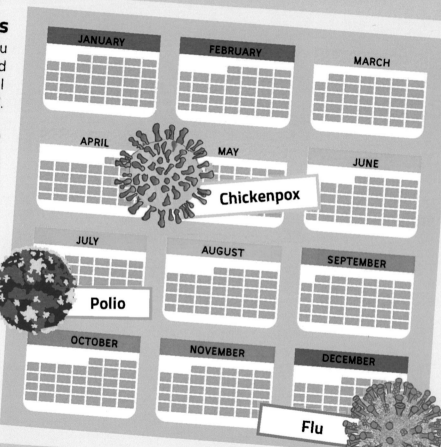

JANUARY FEBRUARY MARCH APRIL MAY JUNE JULY AUGUST SEPTEMBER OCTOBER NOVEMBER DECEMBER

Chickenpox

Polio

Flu

Fast Facts

There are more than 200 different viruses that can cause a common cold or an upper respiratory infection.

Most common viral diseases cause illness for a period of time, then they clear up and symptoms disappear as the immune system attacks the virus and the body recovers.

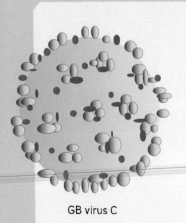

GB virus C

Did you know that most viruses do not cause disease?

As a matter as fact, many viruses co-exist with animals and plants. They help their host to survive and evolve.

Helpful viruses include bacteriophage, adenovirus, ancient retrovirus, gamma-herpesvirus, and pegivirus C or GB virus C (GBV-C).

Who Names Diseases?

The International Classification of Disease (ICD) foundation managed by the World Health Organization (WHO) officially names diseases. Diseases are named to enable discussion on disease prevention, spread, transmissibility, severity, and treatment.

WHO announced "COVID-19" as the name of the new disease caused by SARS-CoV-2 on February 11, 2020.

Infectious Disease Names and Negative Effects

Disease names can have unintended negative effects on countries, economies, communities, and people. Responsible naming of a disease is important to minimize stigmas, stereotypes, violence, or other unwanted actions. With this in mind, the WHO, together with other organizations, developed best practices to naming diseases. These practices supplement the ICD's system as an interim solution to final ICD disease names.

Use specific descriptive terms like time course, age group, severity, or seasonality.

Examples: progressive, juvenile

Use generic descriptive terms such as with symptoms, physiological processes, or systems affected.

Examples: respiratory, enteritis, cardiac

Use the pathogen that caused the disease.

Examples: coronavirus, influenza virus

Use year (+/- month) of first detection or reporting.

Examples: 2019, 12/2019

Use arbitrary identifier.

Examples: alpha, beta.

Avoid names with geographic locations; people's names; species of animal; food or species of animal; cultural, population, industry, or occupational references; and terms that incite undue fear.

Examples: Spanish flu, Chagas disease, bird flu, Legionnaires, unknown or fatal.

How viruses are classified

To study and understand viruses with similar characteristics, scientists use classification systems. Virus classification is the process of naming viruses and placing them into a taxonomic system.

Naming a Virus

In the early years following virus discovery, there were no systems for classifying viruses. Viruses were named in many ways:

Disease Caused
(murine leukemia virus)

Associated Disease
(poliovirus, rabies)

Location
(Sendai virus, Coxsackievirus)

Body Part Infected
(rhinovirus, adenovirus)

Scientists
(Epstein-Barr virus)

Theory of Infection
(dengue = "evil spirit")
(influenza = "influence" of bad air)

Today, viruses are named based on their genetic structure.

Holmes Classification

In 1948, Edward C. Holmes used Carolus Linnaeus's system of assigning a two-part name to classify viruses into three groups based upon the type of host: viruses that attack bacteria, plants, and animals. (This system lacked the consideration for viruses' form and structure similarities.)

Animal Virus
Animal viruses cause dangerous diseases in humans and domestic animals.

Common animal viruses: *poliovirus, vaccinia virus, adenovirus, herpesvirus, reovirus, dengue virus, yellow fever virus, rabies lyssavirus, mumps orthorubulavirus, measles virus, influenza virus, and HIV.*

Plant Virus
Plant viruses are those that cause diseases in plants.

Common plant viruses: *tobacco mosaic virus, tomato mosaic virus, potato virus, papaya mosaic virus, cucumo virus, tobacco necrosis virus, alfalfa mosaic virus, and cauliflower mosaic virus.*

Bacteria Virus
Viruses that infect bacteria are called bacteriophages.

Common bacteriophage:
T4 bacteriophage. The "T" stands for type.

HIV

Cauliflower mosaic virus

T4 bacteriophage

LHT Classification

In the 1960s, scientists began studying viruses under commercially sold electron microscopes. They began to notice that virus particles had different sizes, shapes, and structures. These observations led to new criteria for classification.

Soon after, André Lwoff, Robert Horne, and Paul Tournier (LHT) proposed the LHT system based on a virus's chemical and physical characteristics like nucleic acid (DNA or RNA), symmetry (helical, icosahedral, or complex), presence of envelope, diameter of capsid, and number of capsomers.

electron microscopes

ICTV Classification

Since 1970, this system used a slightly modified version of the standard biological classification system. It categorized organisms using five levels (order, family, subfamily, genus, and species). More recently, the ICTV has changed the system to allow a 15-rank classification that aligns with the Linnaean taxonomic system. This new structure can accommodate the entire spectrum of genetic divergence in the virosphere.

Rank (_suffix)	15-rank structure (2019)	Taxa
		Many

Species (irregular)
Subgenus (_virus)
Genus (_virus)
Subfamily (_virinae)
Family (_viridae)
Suborder (_virineae)
Order (_virales)
Subclass (_viricetidae)
Class (_viricetes)
Subphylum (_viricotina)
Phylum (_viricota)
Subkingdom (_virites)
Kingdom (_virae)
Subrealm (_vira)
Realm (_viria)

Few

Who names viruses?

The International Committee on Taxonomy of Viruses (ICTV). ICTV uses the ICTV Classification System to ease the development of tests, vaccines, and medicines.

Baltimore Classification

The Baltimore system, developed in 1971, is the most commonly used classification system. It classifies viruses into seven groups according to their genome type (DNA or RNA), strandedness (single-stranded (ss) or double-stranded (ds)), and replication method. It was developed by David Baltimore, a virologist and Nobel laureate.

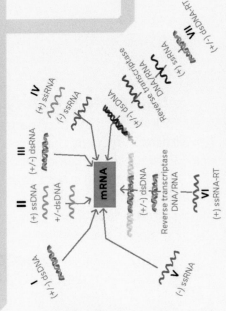

Fast Facts

Although many viruses have been classified, a number of viruses remain unclassified.

- Virus classification is an ongoing process because of the pseudo-living nature of viruses.

- Viruses are notorious to classify because of their wide diversity, high rates of change, and tendency to exchange genetic material.

binds DPP4
binds ACE2
binds APN

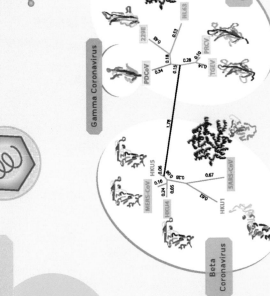

Gamma Coronavirus

Alpha Coronavirus

Beta Coronavirus

Source Credit: Ng WM, Stelfox AJ, Bowden TA. Unraveling virus relationships by structure-based phylogenetic classification. Virus Evol. 2020 Feb 12;6(1):veaa003. doi 10.1093/ve/veaa003. PMID: 32064119; PMCID: PMC7015158.

Structure-based Classification

This emerging structure-based classification system was proposed in 2017 and is based upon the evolutionary relationship between viruses that have similarity in virion assembly and structure for certain viral groups infecting cells from different domains of life (bacteria, eurkarya, archaea). It categorizes viruses with their close relatives. It could complement the ICTV system by classifying newly emerging viruses that cannot be classified under that scheme.

The Baltimore classification system

The Baltimore system is the most commonly used system that classifies viruses that behave in the same manner into groups depending on a combination of their genetic material (DNA or RNA), strandedness (single-stranded (ss) or double-stranded (ds)), and replication method to make mRNA.

Baltimore's Understanding of Viruses

When developing this classification system, Baltimore knew that:

1. Viruses can copy DNA and/or RNA.
2. Viruses can make RNA from DNA (and DNA from RNA).
3. Viruses lack the tools to make proteins.
4. Host cells can make proteins only from positive messenger RNA (mRNA) strands.
5. Viruses rely on cell ribosomes to translate mRNA and make virus copies.

Baltimore's Theory

Baltimore concluded that all viruses must copy their DNA or RNA and make a messenger RNA (mRNA) strand with instructions the cell's ribosomes can read to produce proteins and make more virus.

Group: III

Has both positive and negative RNA strands that correspond and complement mRNA

+/-dsRNA

DNA Viruses

+/-dsDNA

+/-dsDNA

+ssDNA

Group: I

Has both positive and negative DNA strands that correspond and complement mRNA

Group: II

Has a single positive DNA strand and needs to create a negative DNA strand to move to +/-dsDNA, which would correspond and complement mRNA

Baltimore's Solution

Because some viruses have a DNA genome type and some an RNA genome type, they make mRNA in different ways.

To address this, Baltimore grouped viruses into seven categories based on three observations of their genetic material.

RNA Viruses

Group: IV

Has a single positive RNA strand and needs to create a negative RNA strand to move to +/-ssRNA, which would correspond and complement mRNA

Group: V

Has a single negative RNA strand and needs to create a positive RNA strand (+ssRNA) to move to +/-ssRNA, which would correspond and complement mRNA

+ssRNA

-ssRNA

Reverse Transcriptase Viruses

Retroviruses are unique

Has an enzyme called reverse transcriptase, which makes -ssDNA using the positive RNA template

-ssRNA

DNA/RNA Reverse transcriptase

+ssRNA

+/-dsDNA

+/-dsDNA

DNA/RNA Reverse transcriptase

mRNA

+ssRNA-RT with DNA intermediate

Gapped +/-dsDNA-RT

Modeling Baltimore's Classification System

Using the basic cell biology concept "DNA makes RNA makes protein," each virus group takes steps inside the cell's nucleus to transcribe (copy) their DNA or RNA to make messenger RNA (mRNA).

The mRNA then travels outside the nucleus to the cytoplasm to bind with the cell's ribosomes. The cell's ribosomes translate (decode) the mRNA to produce proteins and make virus copies.

Group: VI

Has a single positive RNA strand plus its reverse transcriptase creates negative DNA strand (-ssDNA) in order to then create a +/-dsDNA that corresponds and complements mRNA

Group: VII

Has both positive and negative DNA strands with a gap. This group must fill the gap in order to correspond and complement mRNA

1. Is the genetic material **DNA, RNA,** or **reverse transcribing DNA** or **RNA?**

2. Is the genetic material single-stranded (ss) or double-stranded (ds)?

Single stranded

Double stranded

3. Does the direction of the molecules on the DNA and RNA (base genetic sequence) match the direction of molecules on the mRNA? That is, is the DNA or RNA:

a) corresponding (same direction/ positive)?

b) complementary (opposite direction/ negative)?

c) both corresponding and complementary (same direction/positive and opposite direction/negative)?

Common human viruses

Many viruses are common to humans. Here are some examples of the most common human viruses that cause common diseases. How many have you heard of?

Measles virus (MeV)

Disease: Measles (other names morbilli, rubeola, red measles, English measles)
Year Identified: 854 BCE, estimated emergence in Iran
Infects: Humans
Transmitted: Via contact and airborne droplets
Affects: Respiratory tract
(One of the most contagious infectious diseases in the world; common infection in children)

Human immunodeficiency virus (HIV)

Disease: Acquired immune deficiency syndrome (AIDS)
Year Identified: 1966, Norway, and 1981, United States
Infects: Humans and nonhuman primates
Transmitted: Via contact with bodily fluid
Affects: Body's immune system

HCoV-NL63

Disease: Human coronavirus NL63
Year Identified: 2004, Netherlands, but likely circulated in humans for centuries
Infects: Humans, but originated from infected palm civets and bats
Transmitted: Via droplet-respiration and contaminated objects
Affects: Upper and lower respiratory tracts
(May be associated with Kawasaki disease; found primarily in children, the elderly, and patients with weaker immune systems)

Marburg virus

Disease: Marburg virus disease (MVD)
Year Identified: 1967, Germany
Infects: Humans and nonhuman primates
Transmitted: Via blood and other bodily secretions
Affects: Entire body
(It is considered extremely dangerous)

MERS-CoV (coronavirus)

Disease: Middle East respiratory syndrome (MERS)
Year Identified: 2012, Saudi Arabia
Infects: Humans, bats, and camels
Transmitted: Via respiratory secretions like coughing, but how it spreads is not fully understood
Affects: Respiratory system

Variola virus

Disease: Smallpox
Year Identified: Unknown, worldwide. 3rd c. BCE, possibly imported to China 1157 BCE, dates back to Egyptian mummies
Infects: Humans
Transmitted: Via airborne droplets and direct contact with bodily fluids or contaminated objects
Affects: Respiratory system, eyes, and skin
(Last naturally occurring case diagnosed in 1977. World Health Organization certified global eradication of smallpox in 1980)

HCoV-OC43

Disease: Human coronavirus OC43
Year Identified: Unknown, worldwide. 19th c., thought to have emerged in the context of a pandemic 1960s, first isolated
Infects: Humans and cattle
Transmitted: Via droplet-respiration and contaminated objects
Affects: Lower respiratory tract
(One of the viruses responsible for the common cold; can affect children, the elderly, and patients with weaker immune systems)

Hepatitis B virus

Disease: Hepatitis B
Year Identified: 1965, by Dr. Baruch Blumberg
Infects: Humans
Transmitted: Via contact with infected blood or bodily fluid
Affects: Liver

SARS-CoV-1

Disease: Severe acute respiratory syndrome (SARS)
Year Identified: 2002-2003, emerged in Guangdong province in southern China
Infects: Humans, bats, and civet cats
Transmitted: Via respiratory droplets or contaminated objects
Affects: Respiratory system
(There are ongoing investigations to learn more)

Hantavirus

Disease: Hantavirus pulmonary syndrome (HPS) and hemorrhagic fever with renal syndrome
Year Identified: 12th c., China
Infects: Humans and mice
Transmitted: Via contact with rodent urine, saliva, or feces
Affects: Liver

Influenza A (H5N1)

Disease: Avian influenza "bird flu"
Year Identified: 1997, Hong Kong's poultry population
Infects: Humans and many other animal species
Transmitted: Via birds' saliva, nasal secretions, feces, and blood
Affects: Lower respiratory tract

Influenza A (H3N2)

Disease: 1968 Flu Pandemic (Hong Kong flu)
Year Identified: 1968, Hong Kong
Infects: Birds and mammals and may transmit to humans
Transmitted: Via respiratory droplets
Affects: Respiratory system

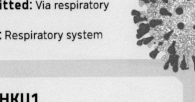

HCoV-HKU1

Disease: Human coronavirus HKU1
Year Identified: 2004-2005, Hong Kong
Infects: Humans and mice
Transmitted: Via droplet-respiration and contaminated objects
Affects: Upper and lower respiratory system

Influenza A (H2N2)

Disease: Influenza flu (Asian or Russian flu)
Year Identified: 1957, Singapore
Infects: Birds and mammals, including humans
Transmitted: Via respiratory droplets
Affects: Respiratory system

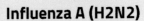

See more viruses on next page

Epstein-Barr virus (human herpesvirus-4 (HHV-4))

Disease: Burkitt lymphoma
Year Identified: Unknown, worldwide. 1964, in a lab by Sir Michael Anthony Epstein and Yvonne Barr
Infects: Humans
Transmitted: Contact with bodily fluids, primarily saliva
Affects: Immune system
(Fatal if not promptly treated)

Rotavirus

Disease: Rotavirus disease
Year Identified: 1973, in children hospitalized with acute diarrhea
Infects: Humans
Transmitted: Via hand-to-mouth contact from contaminated surfaces
Affects: Bowels, stomach and intestines
(Most common cause of diarrhea in infants and children worldwide; highly contagious)

Mumps orthorubulavirus (MuV)

Disease: Mumps
Year Identified: Unknown, worldwide. 1934, in a lab by Claud D. Johnson and Ernest W. Goodpasture
5th c. BCE, first written description found
Infects: Humans
Transmitted: Direct contact, droplet spread, or contaminated objects
Affects: Any part of the body, but mostly the parotid and salivary glands and other tissues

Fast Facts

Viruses, and the diseases they cause, often have different names. People often know the name of a disease, but not the name of the virus that causes it.

●

Together, HCoV-229E and HCoV-OC43 have been responsible for between 10-30% of all common colds since the 1960s.

●

Everyone on the planet is infected with at least one human herpes simplex virus (HSV-1 or HHV-1, HSV-2 or HHV-2, VZV, HCMV, EBV, HHV-6, HHV-7, and HHV-8). The most common are HSV-1 or HHV-1 and HSV-2 or HHV-2. Once you are infected, you are infected for life. Some people develop symptoms, and some do not. It all depends on how well your immune system works.

Influenza A (H1N1)
Disease: Influenza flu (Spanish flu)
Year Identified: 2009, Mexico
Infects: Pigs and some mammals, including humans
Transmitted: Via respiratory droplets and contaminated surface contact
Affects: Lungs

Dengue virus
Disease: Dengue fever
Year Identified: Unknown, worldwide. 1943, in a lab by Ren Kimura and Susumu Hotta, Japan. 265-420 CE, in a Chinese medical encyclopedia from the Jin Dynasty
Infects: Humans and nonhuman primates
Transmitted: Via infected Aedes mosquitoes, particularly A. aegypti mosquitoes
Affects: Blood

HCoV-229E
Disease: Human coronavirus 229E
Year Identified: Unknown, worldwide. 1965, in a lab by Dorothy Hamre, a researcher at University of Chicago
Infects: Humans and bats
Transmitted: Via droplet-respiration and contaminated objects
Affects: Respiratory system
(One of the viruses responsible for the common cold)

Polio virus
Disease: Poliomyelitis
Year Identified: Effects known since pre-history. Scarce occurrences throughout history. Scottish poet Sir Walter Scott contracted polio in 1773
Infects: Humans
Transmitted: Via food, water, person-to-person contact
Affects: Intestine, brain, spinal cord
(Damages motor neurons causing stiffness of neck, convulsion, paralysis of limbs generally legs)

Varicella-Zoster virus (VSZ) aka human herpesvirus 3 (HHV-3)
Disease: Chickenpox
Year Identified: Unknown, worldwide. 1500s, in a history of medicine book by Giovanni Filippo
Infects: Humans
Transmitted: Airborne disease; person-to-person spread via coughs and sneezes
Affects: Skin (rash with small, itchy blisters)
(Primarily affects children. Related adult illness is known as shingles. Highly contagious)

Hepatovirus A
Disease: Hepatitis A (Infectious mononucleosis)
Year Identified: 1973, by Albert Kapikian and Robert Purcell
Infects: Humans and primates
Transmitted: Via inhalation of dried feces or urine from an infected mouse or via contaminated food or water
Affects: Blood

West Nile virus

Disease: West Nile fever
Year Identified: 1996, Morocco
Infects: Humans and birds
Transmitted: Via infected Culex
mosquitoes
Affects: Brain

Ebola virus

Disease: Ebola virus disease (EVD)
Year Identified: 1976, Republic of
Sudan and Democratic Republic
of the Congo
Infects: Humans and other primates
Transmitted: Via contact
with bodily fluids like blood
Affects: Body with hemorrhagic
bleeding internally and externally
(This disease has a high risk of death)

Yellow fever virus

Disease: Yellow fever
Year Identified: Around 1,000
BCE, believed to originate in East
or Central Africa
Infects: Humans, primates,
and several types of mosquitoes
Transmitted: Via A. aegypti
mosquito
Affects: Liver

Zika virus

Disease: Zika fever or Zika virus
disease
Year Identified: 1947, Uganda
Infects: Humans and monkeys
Transmitted: Via infected A.
aegypti mosquitoes, blood
transfusion, sex, or birth
Affects: Brain and nervous system

Chikungunya virus

Disease: Chikungunya
Year Identified: 1952, Tanzania
Infects: Humans and nonhuman
primates
Transmitted: Via infected A. aegypti
and A. albopictus mosquitoes
Affects: Joints

Rabies lyssavirus
(formerly Rabies virus)

Disease: Rabies
Year Identified: 9th c., first described by Persian
physician-philosopher Zakariya Razi
Infects: Humans and other mammals, including bats,
birds, raccoons, skunks, foxes, and coyotes
Transmitted: Via contact with body fluid like saliva
Affects: Central nervous system of the brain and
causes inflammation

Adenovirus

Disease: Adenovirus infection
Year Identified: Unknown,
worldwide. 1953, in a lab by Wallace
Rowe in United States
Infects: Humans, dogs, fowl, mice,
cattle, pigs, and monkeys
Transmitted: Via droplets
Affects: Respiratory system

Rubella virus

Disease: German measles
Year Identified: 1962, by Paul Parkman,
Thomas Weller, and Franklin Neva
Infects: Humans
Transmitted: Via respiratory droplets
Affects: Skin, glands or lymph nodes,
joints, and brain

Rhinovirus

Disease: Common cold
Year Identified: Unknown, worldwide. 1953,
by Winston Price, Johns Hopkins University
Infects: Humans
Transmitted: Via aerosols of respiratory
droplets and from contaminated surfaces,
including direct person-to-person contact
Affects: Upper respiratory tract (the nose),
including the throat, sinuses, and larynx

UNDERSTANDING CORONAVIRUS

What are coronaviruses?

Coronaviruses are a large family of related RNA viruses. They can infect animals and people. Infections are usually associated with intestines or respiratory diseases in their hosts. But, they can also affect the liver, nervous system, and other organs. In humans, coronaviruses mainly cause respiratory diseases ranging from the common cold to pneumonia to more rare and serious diseases, such as severe acute respiratory syndrome (SARS) and Middle East respiratory syndrome (MERS).

Fast Facts

The Coronavidae family gets its name because the virus surface appears like a solar corona under an electron microscope.

Most of us will be infected with a coronavirus at least once in our life.

The first coronavirus was discovered in chickens in the 1930s.

RNA Viruses

Order: Nidovirales

Family: Coronaviridae

Subfamily: Coronavirinae

Genus (type): Coronavirus

Alphacoronavirus

PEDV

TGEV

FIPV

CCoV

PRCV

Betacoronavirus

Lineage A

HCoV-OC43

BCoV

PHEV

AntelopeCoV

Gammacoronavirus

IBV

TCoV

BWCoV-SW1

DCoV

GCoV

Deltacoronavirus

BuCoV HKU11

ThCoV HKU12

MunCoV HKU13

PorCoV HKU15

WECoV HKU16

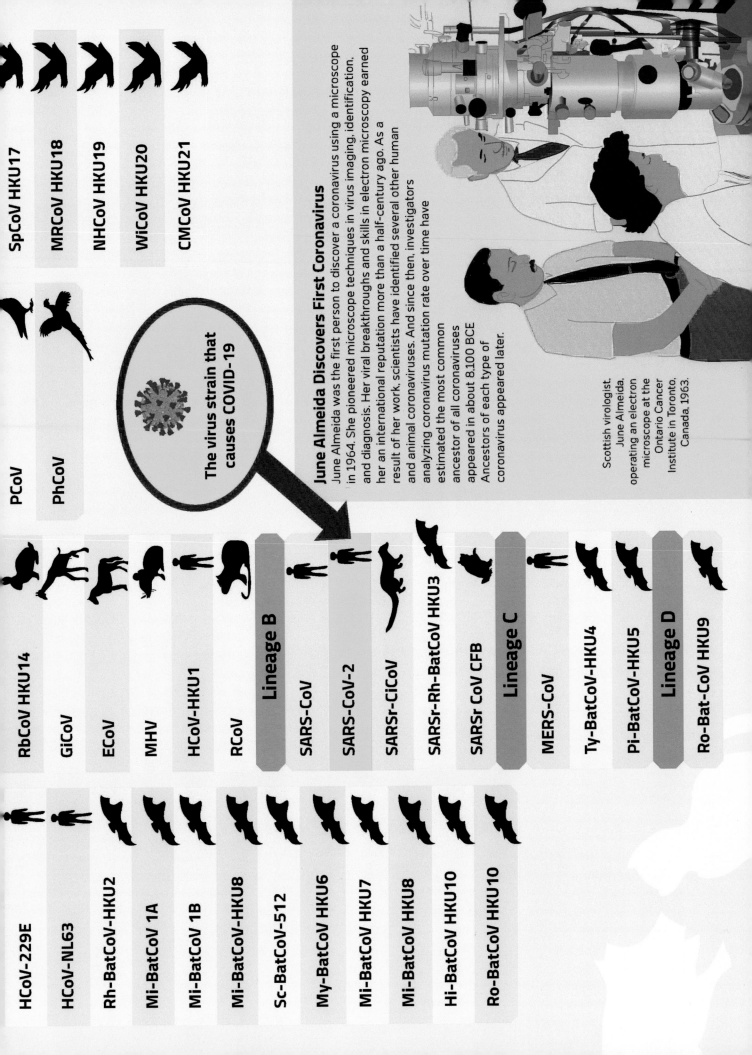

SpCoV HKU17

MRCoV HKU18

NHCoV HKU19

WiCoV HKU20

CMCoV HKU21

PCoV

PhCoV

The virus strain that causes COVID-19

June Almeida Discovers First Coronavirus

June Almeida was the first person to discover a coronavirus using a microscope in 1964. She pioneered microscope techniques in virus imaging, identification, and diagnosis. Her viral breakthroughs and skills in electron microscopy earned her an international reputation more than a half-century ago. As a result of her work, scientists have identified several other human and animal coronaviruses. And since then, investigators analyzing coronavirus mutation rate over time have estimated the most common ancestor of all coronaviruses appeared in about 8,100 BCE Ancestors of each type of coronavirus appeared later.

Scottish virologist, June Almeida, operating an electron microscope at the Ontario Cancer Institute in Toronto, Canada, 1963.

HCoV-229E

HCoV-NL63

Rh-BatCoV-HKU2

Mi-BatCoV 1A

Mi-BatCoV 1B

Mi-BatCoV-HKU8

Sc-BatCoV-512

My-BatCoV HKU6

Mi-BatCoV HKU7

Mi-BatCoV HKU8

Hi-BatCoV HKU10

Ro-BatCoV HKU10

RbCoV HKU14

GiCoV

ECoV

MHV

HCoV-HKU1

RCoV

Lineage B

SARS-CoV

SARS-CoV-2

SARSr-CiCoV

SARSr-Rh-BatCoV HKU3

SARSr CoV CFB

Lineage C

MERS-CoV

Ty-BatCoV-HKU4

Pi-BatCoV-HKU5

Lineage D

Ro-Bat-CoV HKU9

Human coronaviruses

Coronaviruses emerge all around the world. Prior to 2019, there were six known coronaviruses that infect humans: HCoV-229E, HCoV-NL63, HCoV-OC43, HCoV-HKU1, MERS-CoV, and SARS-CoV. As of December 2019, there are now seven human coronaviruses with the emergence of SARS-CoV-2.

The Common Cold and Coronavirus

The four coronaviruses associated with the common cold are: 229E, OC43, NL63, and HKU1. These coronaviruses cause mild disease with less severe symptoms. They are endemic, meaning they regularly emerge among particular people in society, or in a certain area.

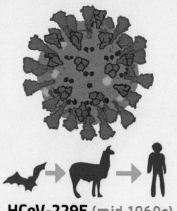

HCoV-229E (mid 1960s)

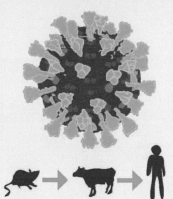

HCoV-OC43 (mid 1960s)

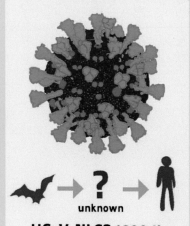

unknown

HCoV-NL63 (2004)

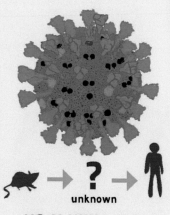

unknown

HCoV-HKU1 (2005)

On their own, 229E and OC43 coronaviruses rarely cause severe disease. But, if a person has co-infection with coronaviruses and other viruses and bacteria, the combination can result in more severe disease.

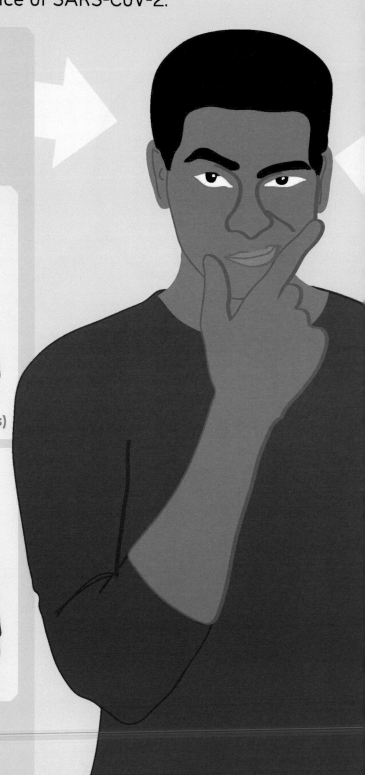

Deadlier Coronavirus Strains

While the first four coronaviruses cause mild respiratory diseases, the other two, SARS-CoV and MERS-CoV, may cause severe to fatal respiratory diseases.

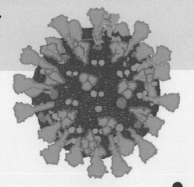

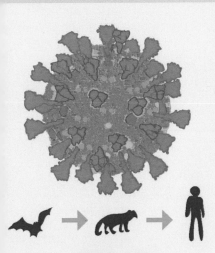

MERS-CoV
Middle East Respiratory Syndrome

In **2012**, another outbreak occurred in Saudi Arabia. This time with a different coronavirus: MERS-CoV. This coronavirus infected dromedary camels and then humans. It is less severe and less contagious than SARS-CoV. Since the first outbreak, there were a few other outbreaks in South Korea in 2015 and again in Saudi Arabia in 2018. Other outbreaks occur each year, but are usually contained.

SARS-CoV
Severe Acute Respiratory Syndrome

First detected in **2002**, SARS-CoV infected civet cats then infected humans. The outbreak of this coronavirus was identified and confirmed in 2003. The last reported case was in 2014.

Fast Facts

The first human coronavirus was identified in the 1960s.

Coronaviruses account for about 10-15% of common colds.

Most coronaviruses occur during the winter months, but the new SARS-CoV-2 occurs any season.

The 7th Human Coronavirus Strain

As of 2019, there are seven coronaviruses. The newest is severe acute respiratory syndrome coronavirus 2, or SARS-CoV-2.

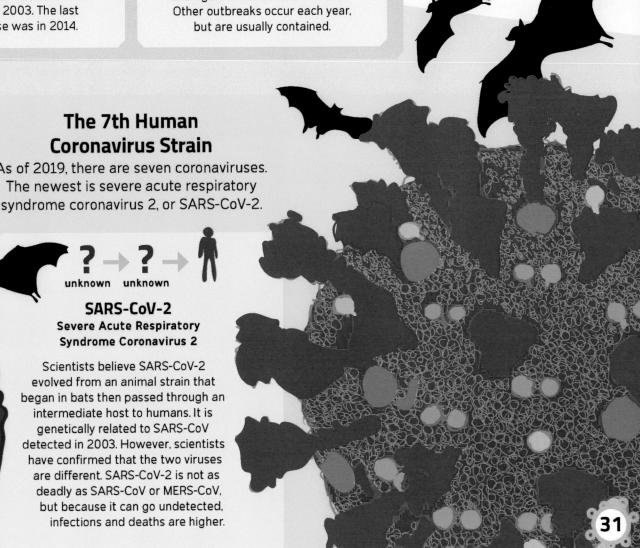

unknown   unknown

SARS-CoV-2
Severe Acute Respiratory Syndrome Coronavirus 2

Scientists believe SARS-CoV-2 evolved from an animal strain that began in bats then passed through an intermediate host to humans. It is genetically related to SARS-CoV detected in 2003. However, scientists have confirmed that the two viruses are different. SARS-CoV-2 is not as deadly as SARS-CoV or MERS-CoV, but because it can go undetected, infections and deaths are higher.

SARS-CoV-2 structure

Like other coronaviruses, SARS-CoV-2 particles are spherical and have proteins called spikes extending from their surface. These spikes attach to a human cell, then fuse with the cell membrane. The virus genes then enter the cell to be copied, producing more viruses.

Capsid
The protein shell of a virus, enclosing its genetic material.

SARS-CoV-2 Anatomy

SARS-CoV-2 has four structural proteins: spike (S) glycoprotein, envelope (E) protein, membrane (M) protein, and nucleocapsid (N) protein. The N protein holds the RNA genome. The S, E, and M proteins together create the viral envelope. The spike protein is the protein responsible for allowing the virus to attach to and fuse with the membrane of a host cell.

Nucleocapsid (N) protein
The primary function of the nucleocapsid is to package the nucleic acid into the capsid.

Nucleic acid
The virus's genetic material consists of a single strand of positive-sense RNA (ribonucleic acid). The RNA stores the instructions for making all the components SARS-CoV-2 needs to multiply.

Fast Facts

The word "coronavirus" comes from the Latin corona, which means crown or halo.

The SARS-CoV-2 Interagency Group (SIG) identifies and actively monitors emerging variants and their potential impact. They group variants in three classes: variants of interest (VOI), variants of concern (VOC), and variants of high consequence (VOHC).

There are countless SARS-CoV-2 variants in circulation, but only a few are causing global concern.

Spike (S) protein
One crucial part of coronavirus is the spike protein. Spike proteins extend from the spherical surface and resemble a crown. The coronavirus uses its spike proteins to attach to and access the membrane of a host cell.

Envelope (E) protein
The envelope is the outermost layer of the virus. It is involved in several aspects of the virus' life cycle, such as assembly, budding, envelope formation, and pathogenesis. It protects the capsid and genetic material in their lifecycle when traveling between host cells.

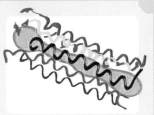

The envelope (E) protein is the smallest of the four structural proteins that make up the SARS-CoV-2 viral particle and is essential for the virus to infect cells.

Hemagglutinin-esterase dimer (HE)
The glycoprotein that is believed to be an invading mechanism to help the virus to infect host cells.

Membrane (M) protein
The membrane protein plays a main role in virus shape development and assembly via its interactions with other viral proteins.

How SARS-CoV-2 Changes
Like other viruses, SARS-CoV-2 mutations are normal and expected. Most mutations are slow with resulting strains being very similar to each other. However, accumulations of mutations can be dangerous. Scientists are concerned that these multiple mutations could be more contagious, deadly, or resistant to vaccines and therapeutics.

Key mutations to the spike protein

Examples of SARS-CoV-2 Variants of Concern (VOC)

Alpha variant B.1.1.7
(a.k.a. 20I (V1)/GRY (formerly GR501Y.V1)
- Earliest samples United Kingdom, September 2020..
- Has an unusually large number of mutations in the receptor binding domain of the spike protein.
- More transmissible (spreads faster and more efficiently).
- May cause more severe illness and increased death.

Beta variant B.1.351
(a.k.a. 20H V2/GH501Y.V2)
- Earliest samples South Africa, May 2020.
- Has multiple mutations in the spike protein.
- Associated with a higher viral load possibly contributing to higher levels of transmission.

Key mutations to the spike protein

Gamma variant P.1
(a.k.a. 20J V3/GR501Y.V3)
- Earliest samples Brazil, November 2020.
- Has 12 unique mutations with several amino acid changes and deletions as well as the spike protein receptor binding domain.
- Believed to be more transmissible.
- May affect antibody ability to neutralize the virus.

Key mutations to the spike protein

Delta variant B.1.617.2
(a.k.a. 21A/G478K.V1)
- Earliest samples India, October 2020.
- Has two mutations that made earlier variants more of a threat.
- May be more transmissible or cause more severe disease, fail to respond to treatment, evade immune response, or fail to be diagnosed by standard tests.

Key mutations to the spike protein

Delta plus variant B.1.617.2.1
(a.k.a. AY.1)
- Delta variant mutation. India, February 2021.

SARS-CoV-2 profile

What should I call it? SARS-CoV-2 or COVID-19? SARS-CoV-2 is the name of the virus that causes coronavirus disease or COVID-19. The acronym COVID-19 means:

CO = corona, VI = virus, D = disease, 19 = year discovered

Recovery:
Mild cases: 2 weeks. Severe cases: 2-6 weeks.

Complications:
Acute pneumonia, respiratory failure, septic shock, multiple organ failure.

Targets:
The primary targets are the lungs, but the virus may also attack the kidneys, heart, intestines, liver, and brain.

Contagious period:
On average SARS-CoV-2 is most contagious in the 2 days before symptom onset.

Incubation period:
2-14 days (typically 5) from infection, though symptoms might appear earlier or later depending on the person.

Virus name:
SARS-CoV-2

Disease:
COVID-19

Size:
50-200 nanometers in diameter.

Transmission:
Transmitted by exposure to virus-infected respiratory fluids spread through air, personal contact via coughs or sneezes from an infected person, or touching infected objects.

Signs & symptoms:
High fever (104 degrees or higher), cough, coughing sputum (a cough that produces mucus or phlegm), shortness of breath, breathing difficulties, fatigue, runny nose, sore throat, loss of appetite, loss of smell, muscle aches, gastro-intestinal symptoms. Many people have low oxygen levels, even when they are feeling well.

Treatments or vaccines:
Several vaccines are available worldwide for emergency use. Many more are under development and testing. Symptoms can be treated as for a cold: drink lots of fluids and build up your immune system.

Severe symptoms:
Pneumonia, severe acute respiratory syndrome, difficulty waking, confusion, bluish face or lips, coughing up blood, persistent chest pain, decreased white blood cells, kidney failure, high fever, death.

Protection & prevention:
Sensitive to ultraviolet rays and heat and can be inactivated by being kept at a temperature of 56 degrees Celsius (133 degrees Fahrenheit) for 30 minutes. It can also be inactivated by solutions like ether, 75% ethanol, and chlorine disinfectants such as bleach. Avoid close unprotected contact. Maintain good hygiene. Wash hands. Wear mask. Avoid touching the face. Stay healthy. Eat well.

Baltimore classification:
Category IV positive single-stranded RNA (+ssRNA) enveloped virus with lipid shell.

Taxonomy type:
Betacoronavirus.

Comparison with SARS-CoV:
More contagious, but less severe.

Fast Facts
It is possible that SARS-CoV-2 can survive freezing temperatures and still be active when thawed.

SARS-CoV-2 proximal origins

SARS-CoV-2 was first recognized in 2019 and spread rapidly worldwide. How did SARS-CoV-2 emerge? The new virus has been studied extensively since its first identification. Yet, many questions about its origins still remain.

Before December 2019

Some studies have suggested that SARS-CoV-2 silently circulated in several countries prior to the first known cases. One study estimated SARS-CoV-2 could have occurred in November 2019.

First Human Cases

In December, 2019, a handful of cases arose at different hospitals in Wuhan City, Hubei province, China. Dr. Li Wenliang, an ophthalmologist, observed a cluster of cases of a deadly pneumonia in patients at the hospital where he worked. His first thought, SARS-CoV was returning. He reported the outbreak to others via an online chat group, but not formally to authorities. Instead, it was Dr. Zhang Jixian who is considered to first report the outbreak to the CDC in Wuhan after observing and isolating patients at the hospital where she worked. Soon after, the CDC in Wuhan issued emergency warnings to local hospitals. Wuhan CDC officials later isolated and confirmed the new virus and identified it as SARS-CoV-2.

Dr. Li Wenliang

WUHAN HUANAN HAIXIAN PIFA SHICHANG

Hunan Market

Some of the infected people were linked to a Wuhan Seafood Wholesale Market, a wet market where people can buy fresh meat, fish, and produce. But, later studies found that it is possible that human-to-human transmission happened prior to this because some infected people had no connection to the market.

Some Proximal Origins Theories

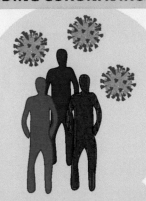

Animal host to human
(natural selection before jumping to humans)

Direct to human

Bat coronavirus have similarities to SARS-CoV-2. Therefore, bats could be a direct to human source of infection and ancestry. The horseshoe bat species (RaTG-13) is ~96% closest to SARS-CoV-2. But, the 4% difference is vast. It may require many years of evolution. In addition, the virus's spike receptor-binding domain (RBD) diverges. This means the virus might not bind well with human ACE2 protein.

Intermediate host to human

Malayan pangolins may be a possible intermediate host to human source of infection. The spike RBD found in these animals have strong similarities to SARS-CoV-2. It is optimized to bind to human ACE2 protein.

Human to human
(natural selection after infection by animal intermediary host)

Human-to-human transmission shows SARS-CoV-2 mutating. Mutations may have taken off, causing the pandemic. Genetic sequencing of SARS-CoV-2 shows features derived from a common ancestor.

Frozen food
products transmission

The WHO team of experts, after investigations, issued a warning of possible SARS-CoV-2 transmission to humans through frozen food products like seafood or meat. Studies show that SARS-CoV-2 "can be carried long distance on cold chain products."

Accidental lab leak
after mutation in lab cell culture

Some believe SARS-CoV-2 mutated in cell culture and possibly escaped by inadvertent infection during the ongoing research on bats. Accidental escape from a lab has been a highly speculative theory. Although lab leaks have happened before with other bacteria and viruses worldwide, they have caused small outbreaks, but never an epidemic. Nonetheless, with all the controversy, this theory continues to remain a mystery.

More Research

The study of SARS-CoV-2's origins is complicated. To date, the true host and location of SARS-CoV-2 is still unknown.

Scientists have not yet found a genetic arrangement that contains the entire virus signature and blueprint together.

It is possible that all hypotheses might be wrong. For example, some studies have shown evidence that the pangolin is not a likely intermediate host animal.

It is possible that there are multiple origins.

It is also possible we may never know the true origin.

As scientists continue to research and collect data on viruses, they may get closer to the full picture of SARS-CoV-2's origins.

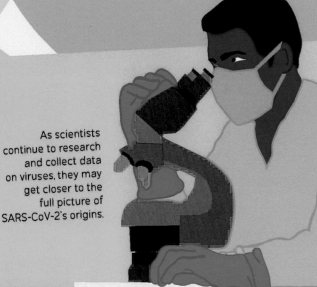

SARS-CoV-2 and human exposure

Who gets infected with SARS-CoV-2? ANYONE can get infected with SARS-CoV-2! People of all ages, races, ethnicities, genders, disabilities, geographies, religions, education levels, income levels, or social rank are at risk. No one is immune. The entire human population is vulnerable. Who gets it depends on the contact they have with SARS-CoV-2 infected people or surfaces.

!

Asymptomatic vs Pre-symptomatic

Many people might confuse asymptomatic with pre-symptomatic. Pre-symptomatic means someone tests positive with the SARS-CoV-2 infection, but does not show COVID-19 symptoms yet. Symptoms may appear as soon as 1 day or as late as 14 days after infection. Most occur in 3 to 7 days. Asymptomatic people test positive with the SARS-CoV-2 infection but never develop COVID-19 symptoms.

What happens when someone gets infected?

If a person gets infected, there are three possible infection statuses: symptomatic, asymptomatic, and pre-symptomatic.

Pre-symptomatic
SARS-CoV-2 + future COVID-19 symptoms

Someone who is pre-symptomatic has tested positive for SARS-CoV-2, but they have not yet developed COVID-19. Their body takes a little longer to show symptoms, so they live their lives normally and might spread the virus to other people unknowingly. People who are pre-symptomatic must take extra precautions to follow public health safety guidelines to avoid infecting others.

Symptomatic=
SARS-CoV-2 + COVID-19 symptoms

Someone is symptomatic when they have the virus infection plus COVID-19 symptoms like fever, body ache, dry cough, and other respiratory problems or illnesses that appear throughout the body. Many people who are symptomatic get better. Their body fights the coronavirus and kills it. Those who do not recover may experience **phases of symptomatic illness.**

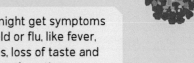

Fast Facts

Asymptomatic or presymptomatic people are estimated to account for more than 50% of SARS-CoV-2 transmissions.

Asymptomatic people can transmit the virus to others for an extended period, perhaps longer than 14 days.

People who are asymptomatic may be more likely to spread the virus because they are less likely to isolate or use preventative measures.

Phases of Symptomatic Illness

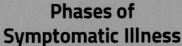

Early Infection Phase
Paucisymptomatic Incubation Period

In this stage the virus has a high level of multiplication inside the body. The immune system engages to fight the virus.

People with a **mild** illness might get symptoms similar to the common cold or flu, like fever, dry cough, aches and pains, loss of taste and smell, stuffy nose, or exhaustion.

T-cell

Cytokines recruite T-cells to hyper amplify proinflammatory cytokine responses

Pulmonary Phase
Nonsevere Symptomatic Illness

The immune system becomes strongly affected by infection. This leads to respiratory symptoms. The body begins to develop T-cells (memory cells) and B-cells (antibodies) to fight the infection.

People with nonsevere symptomatic illness might have persistent coughing, low oxygen levels, high fever, chills, blood clotting, shortness of breath, and be unable to get out of bed. If there is cause for concern, they might need supportive care.

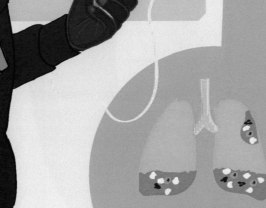

Asymptomatic
SARS-CoV-2 +
no COVID-19 symptoms

A person who is asymptomatic is infected with SARS-CoV-2, but they never develop COVID-19 symptoms.

Hyperinflammatory Phase
Severe Respiratory Illness

At this stage, the immune system hyper-reacts to fight the infection. It causes severe respiratory illness with pneumonia that may or may not lead to respiratory failure. There might also be injury to the heart, kidneys, and other organs. This phase may also demonstrate progressive fever, multi-organ dysfunction, blood thickening, and shock.

Illness may escalate to critical level in individuals with a weaker immune system. Critical patients need hospital attention immediately.

The elderly or people with medical conditions are more vulnerable to developing severe pneumonia or bacterial infections.

Even healthy people can develop severe symptoms.

People with severe conditions might need to use a ventilator machine to help them breathe.

Fluid and cytokines enter infected tissue causing inflammation, leaking, and severe symptoms

39

COVID-19, flu, cold, or allergies?

COVID-19, the flu, the common cold, and allergies have many similar symptoms.

How Do I Know If I have COVID-19 or the Flu?

It may be difficult to tell if you have COVID-19 or the flu since they both have similar symptoms. You might suspect you have COVID-19 if you have respiratory symptoms, you have been exposed to someone who has been infected with SARS-CoV-2, or if there has been community spread of SARS-CoV-2 in your area.

How Is Someone Tested for SARS-CoV-2?

A person may be tested for SARS-CoV-2 using two types of specialized diagnostic tests: molecular (RT-PCR) or antigen (rapid). Both require a nasal swab sample collected from the nasal cavity. The swab must go an inch into the nose to get accurate results. This can be uncomfortable! Luckily, the test only takes about 15 seconds in each nostril. The sample is sent to a facility where the test is performed. The PCR test takes days to over a week for results and is highly accurate. The antigen (rapid) test can produce results in one hour or less, but is considered less accurate.

Fast Facts

A person can be infected with SARS-CoV-2, influenza, or other common cold viruses at the same time because these are different viruses.

Flu
Influenza

Incubation:
around 1-4 days

Common symptoms:
Fever and chills. cough and chest discomfort, muscle pain and body aches.

Occasional symptoms:
Shortness of breath, sinus and ear infections, fatigue, sore throat, nasal congestion. wheezing, diarrhea. nausea, and vomiting.

Complications:
Pneumonia, severe acute respiratory syndrome, heart and brain inflammation, multi-organ failure, sepsis.

Common cold

Rhinovirus, common human coronavirus, respiratory syncytial virus, human parainfluenza virus, adenovirus, human metapneumovirus.

Incubation:
around 1-4 days

Common symptoms:
Sneezing, cough and chest discomfort, nasal congestion, muscle pain and body aches, sore throat, runny or stuffy nose.

Occasional symptoms:
Shortness of breath, loss of smell or taste, fatigue, headache, wheezing, diarrhea. nausea, and vomiting.

Complications:
Pneumonia, severe acute respiratory syndrome mainly in immunocompromised people, especially children and seniors.

Covid 19
SARS-CoV-2

Incubation:
around 1-14 days

Common symptoms:
Fever and chills. cough and chest discomfort, muscle pain and body aches, shortness of breath, loss of small or taste.

Occasional symptoms:
Fatigue, sore throat, headache, nasal congestion. wheezing, diarrhea. nausea, and vomiting.

Complications:
Pneumonia, severe acute respiratory syndrome, heart and brain inflammation, multi-organ failure, sepsis.

When Am I Contagious?
A person infected with SARS-CoV-2 may be contagious 48 to 72 hours before symptoms appear.

How Long Am I Contagious?
A person infected with SARS-CoV-2 is most likely contagious from 48 hours before developing symptoms to 3 days after the last symptoms end.

Can I Get Reinfected?
A person may be infected once with SARS-CoV-2, recover, and later become infected again. Researchers have documented cases in Hong Kong, Europe, and the United States where people have had a second infection several months after their first infection. They were infected with a different strain or variant of SARS-CoV-2.

What does this mean for everyone? It may mean that some people who recover from COVID-19 symptoms and develop an immunity to SARS-CoV-2 may not be fully protected against newer variants of SARS-CoV-2, making them susceptible to reinfection.

Allergies
Airborne allergens (pollen, animal dander, dust mites, mold), certain foods, insect stings, medications, latex or other substances you touch.

Incubation:
several hours after contact

Common symptoms:
Nasal congestion, sneezing, runny nose, itchy/watery eyes, loss of small or taste.

Occasional symptoms:
Cough and chest discomfort, fatigue, shortness of breath, sore throat, headache, wheezing.

Complications:
Severe cases of allergy can progress to bronchitis and pneumonia.

Do Symptomatic and Asymptomatic People Have the Same Amount of Virus?
One study compared the amount of SARS-CoV-2 virus in the nose, throat, and lungs of symptomatic and asymptomatic patients. The results showed that both groups had similar amounts of virus throughout the infection.

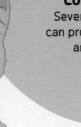

CORONAVIRUS AND THE BODY

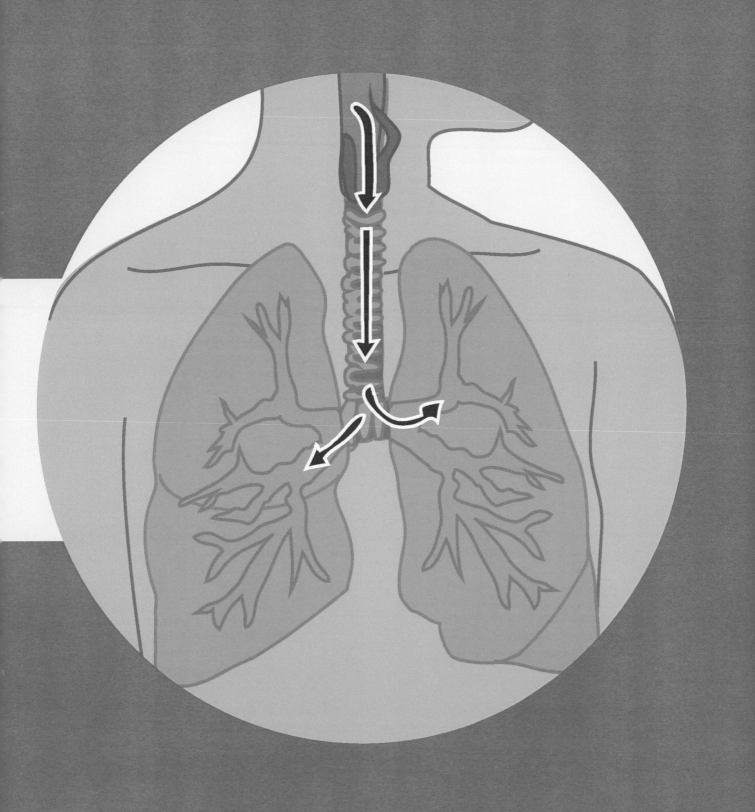

How does SARS-CoV-2 enter the body and cells?

When a person breathes in droplets with SARS-CoV-2 virus particles, they may get infected. The virus particles travel on the person's breath to their goblet and ciliated cells. They then attach to cells via the ACE2 and TMPRSS2 proteins to enter the cell.

1 **Self-Inoculation**
The infection starts when a person self-inoculates with SARS-CoV-2 via the nose, mouth, or eyes.

Upper respiratory tract

Nasal Cavity

Larynx

Pharynx

Lower respiratory tract

Trachea

Bronchi

Lungs

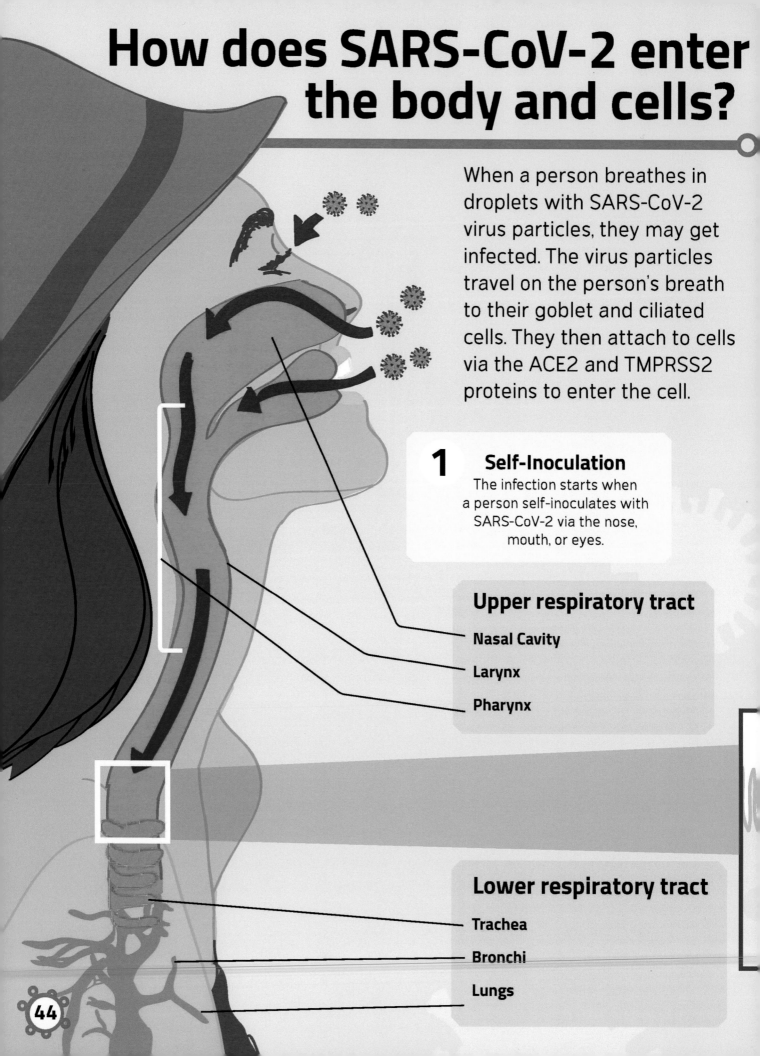

2 Virus to Cell Attraction

Once inside the body, SARS-CoV-2's primary targets are airway epithelial cells, such as ciliated and goblet cells, because of their high expression of ACE2 and TMPRSS2 enzymes. The ACE2 and TMPRSS2 expression levels vary by type, function, and location of the epithelial cell. Expression levels also differ from person to person depending on their age, gender, or comorbidity--the presence of two or more diseases or medical conditions in the same person.

Epithelial cells, like ciliated and goblet cells, are found in many parts of the body like the nasal passage, eyes, trachea, bronchi, lungs, alveoli (air sacs of the lungs), arteries, heart, kidneys, intestines, and other organs.

3 Cell Entry

When the virus reaches a goblet or ciliated cell, it needs one or more receptors and cofactors to get inside the cell. There are two key entry proteins. These are the ACE2 receptor and TMPRSS2 enzymes. The virus uses the combined binding to enter the cell and access its tools to multiply.

The SARS-CoV-2 spike (S) protein attaches to the cell lining of a compatible cell through the ACE2 and TMPRSS2 enzymes.

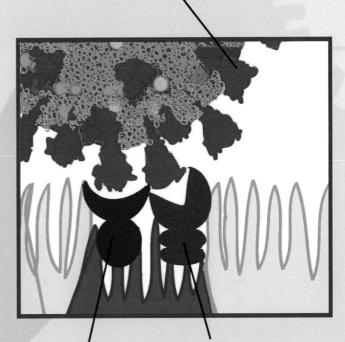

Goblet Cells

Goblet cells are mucus-producing cells that keep the lungs from drying out. Goblet cells also protect the lungs from germs or pathogens—an organism, such as a virus, bacteria, fungi, or parasite that can cause disease.

Ciliated Cells

Ciliated cells push mucus toward the airway, clearing any pathogens from the respiratory tract.

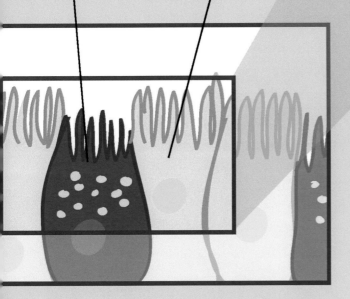

The ACE2 Receptor— The Door to the Cell

SARS-CoV-2 first binds to the angiotensin-converting enzyme 2 (ACE2), which acts as a receptor. ACE2 is an enzyme that generates small proteins that then go on to regulate functions in the cell.

The TMPRSS2— The Entry Facilitator

Once SARS-CoV-2 binds to ACE2, another nearby enzyme named transmembrane serine protease TMPRSS2 adheres to part of the spike protein and activates it. The attachment allows the virus surface to combine with the cell membrane. This lets the virus inside through endocytosis— the cellular process in which substances are brought into a cell.

45

How does SARS-CoV-2 infect and multiply?

Once inside the cell, SARS-CoV-2 uses the cell's machinery to manufacture the components (RNA and proteins) to make copies of itself. As SARS-CoV-2 multiplies, it spreads from the upper respiratory tract (nasal cavity and pharynx) to the lower respiratory tract (lungs) to the alveoli —the lungs' air sacs.

Viral Production

A host cell needs to be both susceptible and permissive for the virus to succeed to establish an infection. Cellular susceptibility requires a cell surface attachment site (receptor) for the virions. To produce more virus particles, a cell also needs to be permissive to infection. That means that the cell needs to have the right intracellular environment that permits virus replication and release.

1

Entry
SARS-CoV-2 attaches to the surface of a target host cell. The spike protein on the virion binds to the ACE2. The TMPRSS2 protein helps the virion to enter the cell.

ACE2 receptor

TMPRSS2

Host Cell

2

Uncoating
The host cell engulfs the virus by endocytosis and fusion.

3

RNA Release
The virion releases its RNA. The replication process begins when SARS-CoV-2 injects RNA instruction into the cell.

Genomic + ssRNA

Ribosomes

Translation

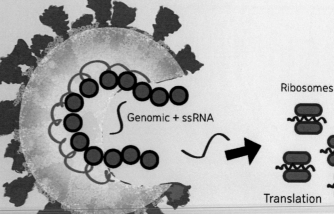
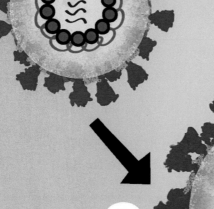

Alveoli

By this stage, the infected person could have a fever, cough, and difficulty breathing. They might even get pneumonia in both lungs.

Viral Load

The viral production damages the infected cells, which eventually die. When that happens, the dead cells shed into the lung airway, clogging the lungs with debris and fluid. The dead cells injure the lining of the respiratory tree—the trachea, bronchi, and bronchioles.

A high viral production will result in more viral particles in the patient's fluids. This is called a high viral load. Viral load, also known as viral burden, is the quantity of viral particles in a given volume of fluid.

4

Transcription

The RNA takes control of the cell. Transcription of the viral RNA originates several mRNAs in the host cell cytoplasm.

7

Release

New viral particles break out of the host cell and infect other cells (exocytosis).

Pre-genomic - ssRNA

RNA Replication

Genomic + ssRNA

Polyproteins

Subgenomic + ssRNA

mRNAs

Golgi Apparatus

5

Translation

The translation machinery of the host cell helps mRNA to produce viral proteins.

6

Assembly

Proteins and RNA are assembled into a new virion in the Golgi.

Nucleus

Endoplasmic Reticulum (ER)

How does SARS-CoV-2 affect the lungs?

As SARS-CoV-2 spreads to the lungs alveoli, the body may or may not develop COVID-19 symptoms. And, the body's immune system begins to fight the infection. If it fails to block the virus, COVID-19 symptoms might escalate, and the lungs may develop acute respiratory distress syndrome (ARDS) or wet lung—a condition in which fluid collects in the lungs' air sacs, depriving organs of oxygen.

1

Immune System Attacks SARS-CoV-2

When cells in the body are under attack by SARS-CoV-2, the body's immune system responds.

During normal immune system function, the inflammation is highly controlled and targets only the infected part of the lungs. In this stage, a person may or may not develop COVID-19 symptoms.

Alveoli laden with macrophages

Macrophages (immune cells) recognize the coronavirus and flood into the lungs to fight the invader. When this happens, the lung tissue becomes inflamed.

Congested capillaries

Neutralized virus

Alveolar

2

Immune System Fails to Contain the Virus and It Spreads

If the immune system fails to silence the virus, a person develops COVID-19. If the immune system cannot contain the infection, it spreads to the lower lungs and into the alveoli.

Inflammation makes the lung alveoli easier for viruses to break into. As a result, fluid leaks into the lungs. This decreases the lungs' ability to push oxygen into the blood and carbon dioxide out of the body. In severe cases, the lungs are flooded with fluid, making it difficult to breathe, and eventually causing severe pneumonia and shortness of breath.

Fluid filled

Loss of alveolar surfactant

Yellow infection

Protein and cellular debris

48

3

Immune System Hyper Reaction

Sometimes, the immune system responds with too many immune cells and they end up destroying healthy lung tissue. This causes further damage to the lungs. This means more cells die and shed in the lungs' airway, adding to the already-clogged space and worsening the pneumonia.

This means more cells die and shed in the lungs' airway, adding to the already clogged space and worsening the pneumonia.

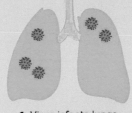

1. Virus infects lungs

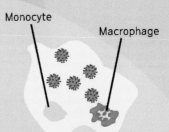

Monocyte

Macrophage

2. Macrophages and monocytes detect virus

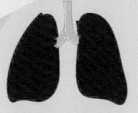

7. Leaking of infected tissue thickens blood into clots and stiffens the lungs

Cytokine Storm Cycle

Around the same time, the immune system hyper reacts and causes another kind of damage. Proteins called cytokines are the immune system's management system, bringing immune cells to the infection site. Overproduction of cytokines can result in a cytokine storm that causes large scale inflammation in the body. Blood vessels widen and become weaker, causing fluids to seep out.

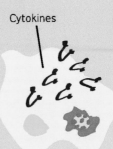

Cytokines

3. Macrophages and monocytes release IL-6 and other proinflammatory cytokines to stimulate immune response

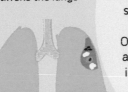

6. Fluid and cytokines enter infected tissue causing inflammation, leaking, and severe symptoms

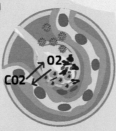

O2

CO2

5. SARS-CoV-2 infects and kills cells. Excess cytokines make blood vessels hyperpenetrable

T-cell

4. Cytokines recruite T-cells to hyper amplify proinflammatory cytokine responses

4

Lung Destruction

Increased damage to the lungs results in respiratory failure. The damage results in scars that stiffen the lungs, causing difficulty breathing. At this stage, a person might need to use a ventilator for breathing. This type of failure may cause permanent lung damage or death.

This makes it more difficult for blood and oxygen to reach the rest of the body, which, in turn, makes it harder to breathe, and eventually leads to hypoxemia or low oxygen levels. If damage continues, in the most severe cases, this can result in multi-organ failure.

The viral load is high in a person whose immune system fails to contain the virus.

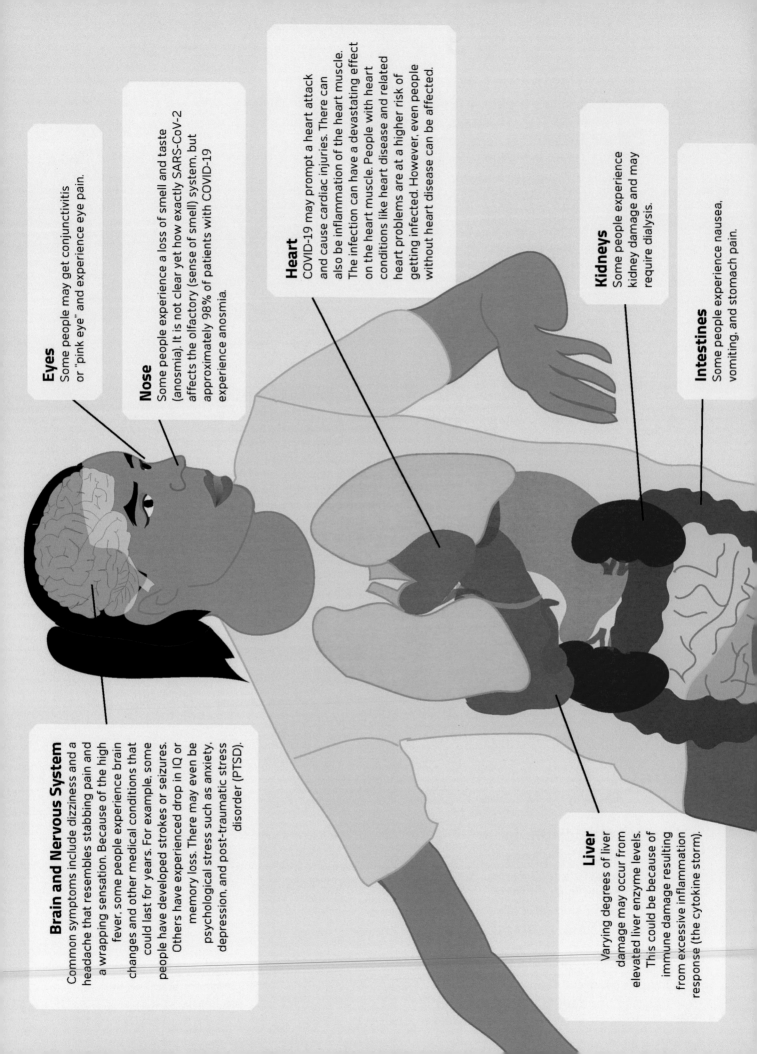

Eyes
Some people may get conjunctivitis or "pink eye" and experience eye pain.

Nose
Some people experience a loss of smell and taste (anosmia). It is not clear yet how exactly SARS-CoV-2 affects the olfactory (sense of smell) system, but approximately 98% of patients with COVID-19 experience anosmia.

Heart
COVID-19 may prompt a heart attack and cause cardiac injuries. There can also be inflammation of the heart muscle. The infection can have a devastating effect on the heart muscle. People with heart conditions like heart disease and related heart problems are at a higher risk of getting infected. However, even people without heart disease can be affected.

Kidneys
Some people experience kidney damage and may require dialysis.

Intestines
Some people experience nausea, vomiting, and stomach pain.

Brain and Nervous System
Common symptoms include dizziness and a headache that resembles stabbing pain and a wrapping sensation. Because of the high fever, some people experience brain changes and other medical conditions that could last for years. For example, some people have developed strokes or seizures. Others have experienced drop in IQ or memory loss. There may even be psychological stress such as anxiety, depression, and post-traumatic stress disorder (PTSD).

Liver
Varying degrees of liver damage may occur from elevated liver enzyme levels. This could be because of immune damage resulting from excessive inflammation response (the cytokine storm).

How does SARS-CoV-2 affect other organs?

The lungs are the most at-risk organs from SARS-CoV-2, but the virus might spread to and infect other areas of the body. It can also enter the gastrointestinal mucosa (stomach), where it reaches the blood and circulatory system. Once the virus reaches the circulatory system, which controls the flow of blood and oxygen in the body, it can also reach other organs. If the cells on that organ have the right receptors (such as ACE2) they are vulnerable to the virus.

Blood

People who have COVID-19 may develop blood clots. Some doctors have treated patients who show mysterious symptoms, like micro clots in the lungs and legs, kidneys, liver, heart, intestines, and brain. Others have half their normal blood oxygen levels (hypoxemia) or abrupt loss of heart function (cardiac arrest) when they had no signs of heart disease.

Skin

The largest organ in the body, the skin, may show red rashes with a lacy pattern, hives, or small blisters. Some people may develop lesions called "COVID-19 toes." Other skin conditions may be tiny burst blood vessels, purple discoloration, and Kawasaki disease—a syndrome of unknown cause that results in a fever from blood vessels becoming inflamed throughout the body.

Fat Cells (Adipose Tissue)

People who have a high rate of body fat are more at risk of contracting infection and possibly ending up on a ventilator.

Muscles and Joints

Some people experience muscle pain and cramps, along with joint pain.

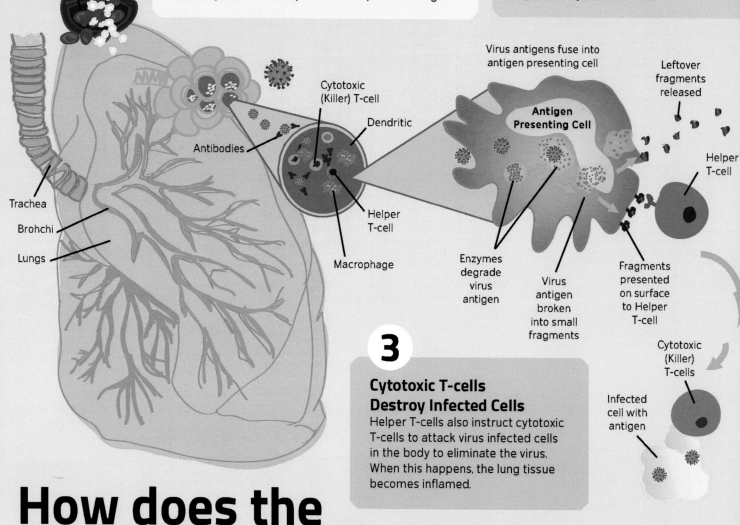

1

Immune System Responds to SARS-CoV-2
When cells are hijacked by SARS-CoV-2 invaders, the immune system responds to fight the infection.

Red and white blood cells prepare defense. Red blood cells move oxygen to tissues and the organs, while white blood cells (immune cells) fight infection.

White blood cells are made up many different cells but monocytes (dendritic cells and macrophage cells), B-lymphocytes (B-cells), and T-lymphocytes (helper T-cells, cytotoxic T-cells) are most important to fight.

2

A. Antigen Presenting Cells Break the Virus into Fragments
At the initial stages, immune response is triggered by activation of antigen-presenting cells, including macrophages and dendritic cells. Macrophages stand guard against SARS-CoV-2 and flood into the lungs to swallow up invaders. They identify parts of the virus called antigens—substances that trigger helper and cytotoxic T-cells.

LOWER RESPIRATORY TRACT

Red and white blood cells

Trachea

Brohchi

Lungs

Cytotoxic (Killer) T-cell

Dendritic

Antibodies

Helper T-cell

Macrophage

Virus antigens fuse into antigen presenting cell

Leftover fragments released

Antigen Presenting Cell

Helper T-cell

Enzymes degrade virus antigen

Virus antigen broken into small fragments

Fragments presented on surface to Helper T-cell

Cytotoxic (Killer) T-cells

Infected cell with antigen

3

Cytotoxic T-cells Destroy Infected Cells
Helper T-cells also instruct cytotoxic T-cells to attack virus infected cells in the body to eliminate the virus. When this happens, the lung tissue becomes inflamed.

How does the body fight SARS-CoV-2?

As SARS-CoV-2 spreads from the upper to lower respiratory tract, if the body has a strong immune system, the body's immune system responds to fight the virus. If it is successful in silencing the virus, the infected person might recover normally and develop antibodies. After recovery, a person may not experience any other COVID-19 effects, or they may continue to show lingering symptoms.

During normal immune system function, the inflammation is highly controlled and targets only the infected part of the lungs. In this stage, a person may or may not develop COVID-19 symptoms. It can take the body several days to clear the infection.

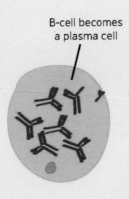

Neutralized virus

B. B-cells Produce Antibodies

Macrophages and dendritic cells see antigens as dangerous and instructs helper T-cells to tell B-cells to start making antibodies. The body then sends the antibodies to neutralize the antigens.

B-cell becomes a plasma cell

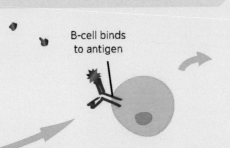

B-cell binds to antigen

Secreted antibodies

Antibodies bind to the virus antigens to prevent the virus from attaching to host cells.

IMMUNE RESPONSE

Memory Helper T-cells

Memory Cytotoxic (Killer) T-cells

Memory B-cells

5 Immune System Deploys Memory Cells

The immune system remembers what it learned about how to protect the body against the virus by producing memory cells from T-lymphocytes. If the person is infected by the same virus again, memory cells jump into action.

4 Immune System Silences the Virus

If the immune system succeeds in fighting the virus, it clears the lungs and repairs the lung tissue to make the person well again.

The viral load in a person whose immune system silences the virus is low to none.

6 Recovery and Post-Effects

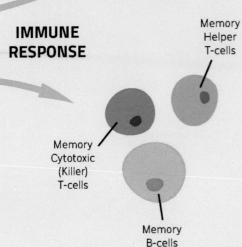

Post COVID-19

Some people who recover from COVID-19 resulting from SARS-CoV-2 strain or variant infection have immunity to the same strain or variant that may last several months. However, the antibodies in recovered patients are said to be generally low. Scientists nevertheless view the presence of antibodies in many recovered patients as a positive sign for vaccine development.

Long Haulers

About a third of patients who recover from COVID-19, whether the illness was mild, moderate, or severe, go on to experience long-term lingering symptoms. These patients are identified as "long haulers" with post-acute COVID-19 syndrome. The infection post-effects can affect multiple organs producing physical symptoms like dizziness, fatigue, and body aches weeks or even months after their initial recovery.

Fast Facts

People who recover from SARS-CoV-2 infection can get reinfected. Subsequently, their immune system may respond faster to fighting the virus.

Other terms for "post-acute COVID-19 syndrome" include "long haulers," "long COVID," and "post-COVID syndrome."

The rate of occurrence, collection of facts, and cause of the symptoms for post-acute COVID-19 syndrome is still a mystery to scientists.

Long haulers and post-COVID-19 syndrome

A number of people who were infected with SARS-CoV-2, developed COVID-19, and recovered experience post-COVID-19 syndrome, a multi-system disease associated with ongoing symptoms and complications like organ damage.

Chest pain

Gastrointestinal upset

Abdominal pain

Neurocognitive difficulties (like brain fog)

Insomnia

Dizziness

Headaches

Thromboembolic conditions (the blocking of a blood vessel by a particle that has broken away from a blood clot)

Shortness of breath or difficulty breathing

Anxiety

Hypertension (high blood pressure)

Heart arrhythmia (irregular heartbeat)

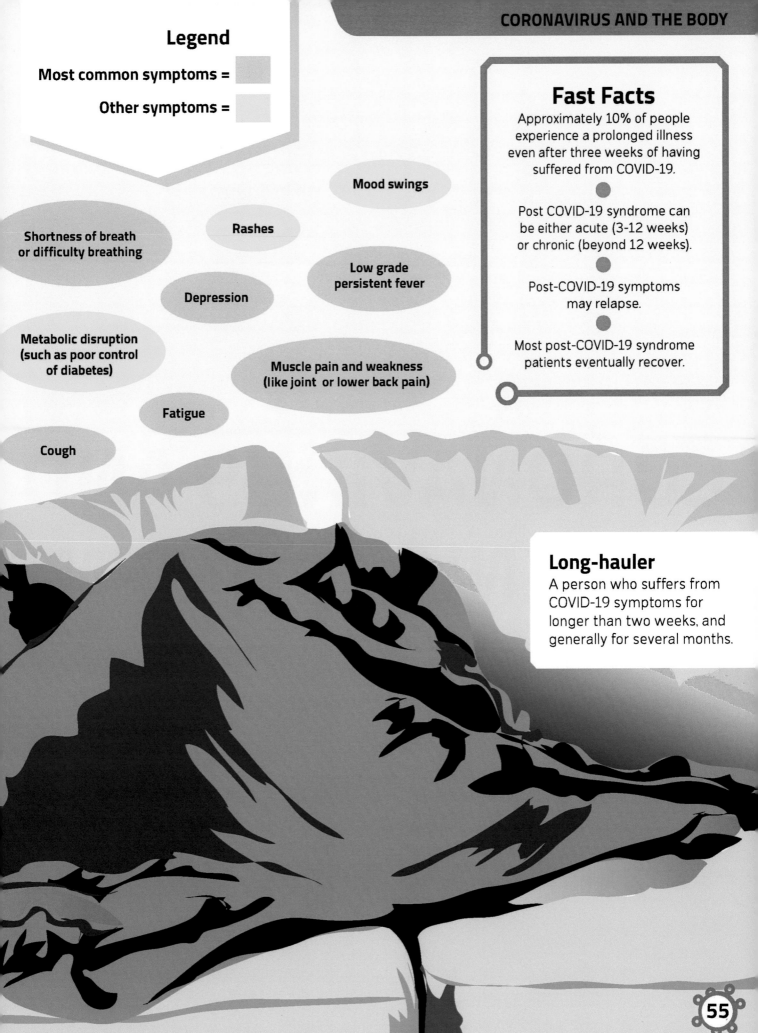

Legend

Most common symptoms =

Other symptoms =

Mood swings

Rashes

Shortness of breath or difficulty breathing

Low grade persistent fever

Depression

Metabolic disruption (such as poor control of diabetes)

Muscle pain and weakness (like joint or lower back pain)

Fatigue

Cough

Fast Facts

Approximately 10% of people experience a prolonged illness even after three weeks of having suffered from COVID-19.

Post COVID-19 syndrome can be either acute (3-12 weeks) or chronic (beyond 12 weeks).

Post-COVID-19 symptoms may relapse.

Most post-COVID-19 syndrome patients eventually recover.

Long-hauler

A person who suffers from COVID-19 symptoms for longer than two weeks, and generally for several months.

CORONAVIRUS AND THE ENVIRONMENT

SARS-CoV-2 person-to-person spread

SARS-CoV-2 spreads mainly through person-to-person contact via respiratory droplets.

Person-to-Person Spread

Coronavirus is thought to spread mainly from person to person. Spread can happen when a noninfected person stands within about 6 feet of an infected person. When the infected person speaks, sings, coughs, or sneezes, respiratory droplets can land on the noninfected person's mouth, nose, or eyes. The respiratory droplet might even be inhaled into the lungs.

Viral Load

Viral load is the amount of virus in the body. Scientists have shown that symptomatic people have a high viral load and therefore can easily spread the virus to other noninfected people. Research shows that an asymptomatic person has the same amount of viral load and can also spread the virus to noninfected people just as much.

Is SARS-CoV-2 Airborne?

The Center for Disease Control (CDC) has confirmed that SARS-CoV-2 is airborne. That means there is a strong possibility of aerosol transmission. This can happen anywhere, but is more likely in closed environments with high concentrations of aerosol.

Droplet Types

Coronavirus primarily spreads through large droplets. The virus can also spread through smaller aerosol droplets called droplet nuclei.

Large droplets

Droplets larger than 5 microns are too heavy to go far and can only travel 1 meter (3.28 feet). They then settle on surfaces.

When Does Spread Happen?

Spread is thought to be the most contagious when people are the sickest, having the most symptoms. It is possible, though, to spread SARS-CoV-2 before showing symptoms.

How Easily Can SARS-CoV-2 Spread from Person to Person?

The ease of spread of a virus varies from virus to virus. Some viruses may spread easily while others take longer. SARS-CoV-2 spreads more easily than the flu, but not as quickly as measles. Virus spread can also be sustained—which means the virus continues to spread beyond just clusters of patients.

Fast Facts

Particles can stay in air droplets up to 3 hours after an infected person speaks, coughs, or sneezes.

How far does a sneeze travel? Studies show a sneeze can produce approximately 40,000 rapidly propelled droplets that might travel up to 7-8 meters (26 feet).

Some evidence even found coronavirus in feces and urine, making environmental pollution by feces and urine a possible aerosol or contact transmission.

Aerosols (Droplet Nuclei)
Aerosols are small droplet nuclei that mix with large droplets in the air. They float for long distances and cause infection after inhaling. Droplet nuclei are smaller than 5 microns and travel longer distances than large droplets.

1 meter
3.28 feet

2 meters
6.56 feet

Delta Variant Spread Example

▶ Higher viral load than prior related variants

▶ Vaccines prevent >90% of severe disease, but may be less effective at preventing Delta infection or spread

▶ People vaccinated and infected with the Delta variant may be as transmissible as people unvaccinated and infected

▶ Highly contagious and likely more severe than previous variants

▶ Spread compared to other viruses:

Virus	Disease	R0
SARS-CoV	SARS	~0.19 to 1.08
MERS-CoV	MERS	~0.3 to 0.8
Seasonal influenza	Seasonal flu	~0.9 to 2.1
1918 influenza	1918 flu	~1.4 to 2.8
Ebola virus	Ebola virus disease	~1.56 to 1.9
Common cold viruses	Common cold	~2 to 3
Variola virus	Smallpox	~3.5 to 6
Varicella-Zoster virus	Chickenpox	~9 to 12
Delta variant	COVID-19	~5 to 8 (each infected person can infect five to eight others)

The R number

Scientists use a technique called R naught (R0) to estimate how many other people might get infected by one sick person. This refers to the effective reproduction number and is a way to measure an infectious disease's ability to spread. It's not a fixed number. It is affected by several factors: how the disease develops over time, population density, life expectancy, demographics, climate, and immunity from infection or vaccination.

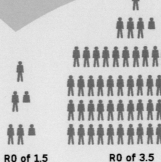

R0 of 1.5   R0 of 3.5

The R0 of SARS-CoV-2 is estimated to be 1.5 to 3.5, which means that for every one person infected, that person can infect 1.5 to 3.5 other people. Officials aim for an R0 below 1.0 by using social and economic restrictions. Below 1 means that the spread of the virus can be paused. It might also die out in a population.

SARS-CoV-2 and other transmission routes

Although people to people is the most common way for SARS-CoV-2 to spread, there are other ways the virus travels. Sometimes it spreads through people to animals. It also spreads via surface contact.

People-to-Animals Spread

Scientists have found that people can spread SARS-CoV-2 to animals such as dogs and cats through close contact. Many studies have been done to show that cats, dogs, ferrets, fruit bats, hamsters, tree shrews, rhesus macaques, cynomolgus macaques, grivets, and common marmosets can become infected with the virus. More studies are needed to understand people-to-animal spread.

The first United States case of animals testing positive from exposure to people happened in tigers and lions at the Bronx Zoo in New York.

Surface Spread

Surface contact transmission may happen when SARS-CoV-2 is spread through a certain surface.
If a noninfected person touches a contaminated surface within the time that the virus is still active, the noninfected person might get infected when they touch their mouth, nose, broken skin, or eyes. Droplets can stay on …

Paper and tissue
3 hours

Copper
4 hours

Cardboard surfaces
24 hours

Animal-to-People Spread

Based upon limited information available to date, spread from animals to people is considered low. But until more is known, the CDC recommends treating pets like human family members to protect them from infection. If your pet becomes sick, or you have questions about your pet's health, a veterinarian can assist with any treatment and care.

Infection has been reported in dogs in several countries and the United States. Nearly all dog infections were due to exposure to an infected person.

In another case of animal infection, minks at mink farms in several countries were infected. The farms suspect farm workers were the initial source of the mink infections. Once one mink is infected, spread can happen between mink and from mink to other animals. This type of animal-to-animal transmission has also been seen in other animals. One study shows that cats can infect each other, but may not have any symptoms.

Fast Facts

Based upon a small number of animals tested, results from studies show that laboratory mice, pigs, chickens, and ducks do not seem to become infected or spread the infection.

There are about 95 million house cats in the U.S. and about 60 million to 100 million feral cats.

There are vaccine programs in testing for animals.

Wood
2 days

Stainless steel
2/3 days

Plastic
2/3 days

Cloth
2 days

Glass and paper money
4 days

Surgical mask
(The outside of)
7 days

SARS-CoV-2 spread in the community

Isolation helps to contain the spread of disease.
One person can bring infection to their community.

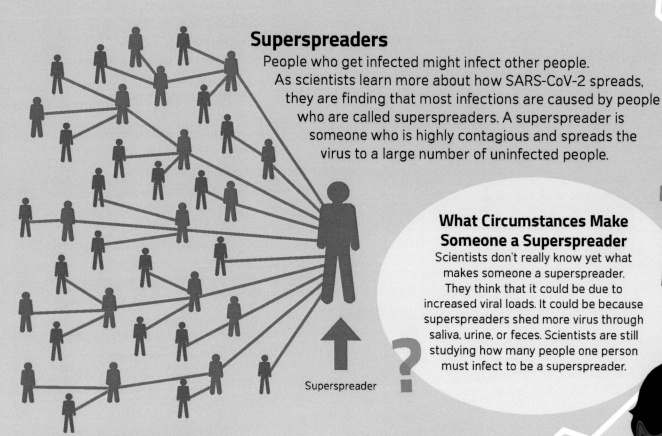

Superspreaders

People who get infected might infect other people.
As scientists learn more about how SARS-CoV-2 spreads,
they are finding that most infections are caused by people
who are called superspreaders. A superspreader is
someone who is highly contagious and spreads the
virus to a large number of uninfected people.

Superspreader

What Circumstances Make Someone a Superspreader

Scientists don't really know yet what
makes someone a superspreader.
They think that it could be due to
increased viral loads. It could be because
superspreaders shed more virus through
saliva, urine, or feces. Scientists are still
studying how many people one person
must infect to be a superspreader.

Contact Tracing

Since there is no way yet to identify
superspreaders, scientists use detective-
like methods called *contact tracing* to
limit further infection. Contact tracing is
when scientists identify infected people,
isolate them, and then isolate the people
they came in contact with. This keeps
superspreaders from moving around and
spreading the virus to other people.

Step 1
Individual tested
and found positive;
person isolates

Step 2
Contacts contacted
and tested

Step 3
Positive contacts
isolate

Next steps
Steps 2 and 3
continued

Last step
No more cases once
contact tracing catches
up with the spreading

What Is Community Spread?

Scientists are also concerned about community spread, or the spread of a contagious disease where the source of infection is unknown. In other words, community spread happens when some people in a specific location have been infected and they:

Have not been in contact with others who were infected,

Have not recently traveled to a place with other infected people.

Are not sure how they became infected.

Public Health
Local health departments determine community spread based on the conditions in their local area.

Herd Immunity by Infection

When a large part of the population of people becomes immune to infection through previous natural infections, it reduces the chances of infection for people who lack immunity. It is believed that to reach this level of protection, 60% to 80% of the population would need to have natural antibodies.

Key

Infected person   Uninfected person   deceased person

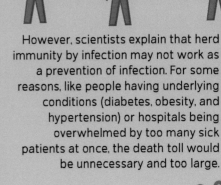

However, scientists explain that herd immunity by infection may not work as a prevention of infection. For some reasons, like people having underlying conditions (diabetes, obesity, and hypertension) or hospitals being overwhelmed by too many sick patients at once, the death toll would be unnecessary and too large.

How did COVID-19 become a pandemic?

Epidemiologists are scientists who study the rates of diseases in populations. They label the spread of an infectious disease using levels: outbreak, epidemic, and pandemic. These levels measure the number of people ill with a disease (evolution), and how far it has spread.

Epidemic and Seasonal Flu
The seasonal flu behaves like an epidemic because the number of people infected suddenly and rapidly increases at different times of the year.

EPIDEMIC

When COVID-19 was limited to Wuhan, China, it was an epidemic.

An outbreak quickly becomes an epidemic when a disease actively, suddenly, and rapidly affects many people in the same community, population, or region. New, local cases of the disease exceed what is normally expected.

Epidemic examples:
Yellow fever, cholera, malaria, SARS, MERS, Ebola virus disease, London flu, smallpox, influenza flu (H1N1)

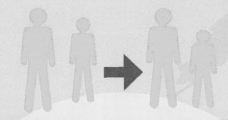

OUTBREAK

With SARS-CoV-2, multiple people in a community got infected and went to a doctor, who noticed an unusually high number of patients with pneumonia. When investigated further, the doctor learned that the disease (named COVID-19) was something new spreading in the community.

Anyone infected with a disease might travel and pass it to other people in a noninfected community. Scientists call the infections in a new community an outbreak—a sudden, big occurrence of a disease.

Outbreak examples:
Dengue fever, Zika fever

Syndemic
Scientists believe that the world is currently experiencing a syndemic with COVID-19 plus other deadly diseases.

A syndemic or synergistic epidemic is the collection of two or more coinciding epidemics or health problems in a population with biological interactions that worsen the burden of a disease in a population.

Infection Frequency

An infection or disease can be sporadic (infrequent) endemic (always present), or hyperendemic (high and persistent).

ENDEMIC

Scientist's believe that COVID-19 might become an endemic that the world will have to learn to live with.

An endemic is when a disease regularly recurs in a specific area or location over and over again. It has a constant presence within that specific location or population. The number of cases do not increase or decrease over time. It remains steady. The number of people affected is low, and the outcome is predictable.

Endemic examples:
Chicken pox, malaria, AIDS, and tuberculosis

PANDEMIC

On March 11, 2020, the World Health Organization declared COVID-19 a pandemic.

What is a pandemic? A pandemic is a widespread disease that affects a significant number of people over multiple countries or continents. Pandemics arise when people travel outside their country to other countries and continents and infect other people.

Another way pandemics can arise is when a virus mutates to a different strain. Virus mutations could infect the same people or other people in other locations, because it is now different. When the mutations infections go global, the epidemic is raised to a pandemic level.

Pandemic examples:
AIDS, influenza flu (H1N1), bubonic plague, COVID-19

Multi-demic
A disease can be more than one level at the same time. Right now, AIDS is a pandemic and an endemic. In the early days of the disease, it was a pandemic and epidemic because of the spiking cases.

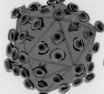

Fast Facts

The place where an epidemic or pandemic originates is called the epicenter of a disease.

•

The words epidemic and pandemic come from the Greek words "epidemia" and "pandemos." Epi means "among," pan means "all, every, whole," and demos means "people."

Pandemics of the past

The world has experienced other pandemics in the past.

c.3 BCE–1967

Smallpox

(Variola virus)

▶ 300–500 million estimated deaths in the 20th c.

▶ 3 out of 10 people who got it died, and those who survived were usually left with scars.

▶ A safe vaccine was created and a global effort to end smallpox was so successful that the virus disappeared.

Edward Jenner, Smallpox vaccine creator.

1520–unknown

New World Smallpox

(Variola Major Virus)

▶ 25–55 million estimated deaths

▶ 90 percent or more of the new world population (Native Americans and First Nations peoples) perished.

▶ No effective anti-viral therapies were available at the time.

1665–1666

Great Plague of London

(Bubonic Plague; Yersinia Pestis Bacteria)

▶ 75,000–over 100,000 estimated deaths

▶ According to the National Archives, "Watchmen locked and kept guard over infected houses. Parish officials provided food. Searchers looked for dead bodies and took them at night to plague pits for burial."

▶ There were no treatments.

1855–1960

The Third Plague

(Bubonic Plague; Yersinia Pestis Bacteria)

▶ 12–15 million estimated deaths

c.7 BCE 500BCE 1300s 1500s 1600s 1800s

c.7 BCE–1963

Measles

(Measles virus)

▶ 200 million estimated deaths

▶ There is a vaccine available.

165–180 BCE

Antonine Plague

(Unknown; suspected Smallpox and Measles)

▶ 5 million estimated deaths

1347–1352

The Black Death

(Bubonic Plague; Yersinia Pestis Bacteria)

▶ 75–200 million estimated deaths

▶ People had no scientific understanding of the Black Death, but they knew proximity was important. They isolated new sailors until it could be proven that they were not sick.

1817–1861

Cholera

(V. Cholera Bacteria)

▶ Seven pandemics from 1817-1961

▶ Over 40 million estimated deaths

▶ It is still an endemic in many countries.

▶ During the Third Cholera pandemic, British Doctor John Snow charted the infected locations to a city well providing drinking water. Making the well unusable made infections disappear. This effort led to improved sanitation and protecting drinking water from contamination.

▶ There is a vaccine available.

541–542 BCE

Plague of Justinian

(Bubonic Plague; Yersinia Pestis Bacteria)

▶ 30–50 million estimated deaths

▶ There is still no understanding how to fight the plague other than to avoid sick people. Scientists' best guess about how it ended is that most people survived and developed immunity.

Late 1800s

Yellow Fever

(Yellow Fever Virus)

▶ *100,000–150,000 estimated deaths*

1968–1970

Hong Kong Flu

(Influenza A, H3N2)

▶ *1 million estimated deaths*
▶ *There is a vaccine available.*

1981–Present

AIDS

(Human Immunodeficiency Virus)

▶ *Over 36 million estimated deaths*
▶ *Over 30 million cases still prevalent around the world*
▶ *There is no vaccine.*

Spanish Flu

(Influenza A, H1N1)

1918–1919

▶ *40–50 million estimated deaths*
▶ *It was one of the deadliest pandemics in human history.*
▶ *Isolations and quarantines were used to slow the transmission. Nobody really knows how it ended, but some scientists believe that the virus mutated to a less lethal strain, which is very common for influenza viruses.*
▶ *There is a vaccine available.*

2000s

1970s

2009

Swine Flu

(Influenza, H1N1)

▶ *200,000 estimated deaths*
▶ *There is a vaccine available.*

1950s

1900s　　**1920s**

1889–1890

Asiatic or Russian Flu

(Uncertain; Influenza A, H3N8, H2N2, or Coronavirus OC43)

▶ *1 million estimated deaths*
▶ *It ended when most of the population became immune to it.*
▶ *There is no vaccine.*

1957–1958

Asian Flu

(Influenza A, H2N2)

▶ *1–2 million estimated deaths*
▶ *It mutated by antigenic shift into H3N2, which caused a milder pandemic.*
▶ *There is a vaccine available.*

Fast Facts

Ring around the rosie, a pocket full of posie. Legend has it that the "Ring Around the Rosie" children's rhyme may have been inspired by the Black Death plague's rash-like rings and ashes of dead victims.

The 1918 flu did not originate from Spain. The "Spanish flu" name was adopted when the flu pandemic reached Spain, the same time the world first learned about the disease.

Legend

Virus =

Bacteria = ▶

How do pandemics end?

According to historians, pandemics end in two different ways. The "medical ending" is when incidence and death rates decline. The "social ending" is when the population no longer fears the virus. With medical endings, the development of vaccines or effective treatments are key to stopping the virus and diseases.

A Medical Ending

One disease with a medical end is smallpox, caused by the variola major virus, which has an effective vaccine with lifelong protection.

Other helpful medical factors include having noticeable symptoms for easy contact tracing and quarantining, or having no animal host.

With vaccines for SARS-CoV-2 and therapeutic developments for COVID-19, public health officials and private companies light a direction toward a medical end.

How Did Some Past Pandemics, Epidemics, and Outbreaks End?

Past pandemics, epidemics, and outbreaks have ended in a variety of ways.

Influenza (Spanish Flu)
Infection control practices were put in place. These included social/physical distancing (avoiding the sick/infected); quarantine (isolating the sick/infected); closing schools, churches, and theatres; limiting large gatherings; flattening the curve; and wearing face masks.

In addition to the possibility that people became immune, the virus may have faded away by evolving into a benign flu. A virus may mutate and die out by itself, either through mutation of the virus to a less lethal strain or because it stops spreading.

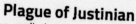

Plague of Justinian
No one really knows how this plague ended, but historians guess that survivors developed immunity. The population may have developed herd immunity, where enough people are widely exposed to a virus and develop immunity against infection.

Black Death
Isolation and quarantine helped to identify the sick. Since then, therapies such as antiserum and antimicrobial drugs have been developed to cure the bubonic plague. Good public health practices like improved sanitation lessened infections.

The Great Plague of London
The sick were confined to their homes, and the dead were buried in mass graves to prevent others from getting sick

A Social Ending

A social ending for a pandemic occurs when fear and anxiety decrease, and people adjust their lives around a disease. Fear can have harmful effects on the vulnerable, even in places without high infection rates.

•

Social psychological frustration and exhaustion may be complicated by other issues like race, ethnicity, and socioeconomic status. As a result, preparations to handle fear and lack of knowledge become as important as fighting a virus and disease.

•

Social endings can be seen with HIV/AIDS and influenza/flu, even though these viruses/diseases are endemic to many countries.

SARS-COV-2 and Social Ending

SARS-CoV-2/COVID-19 encounters a tug of war to a social ending. Early on in the pandemic some members of the public grew frustrated and tired of restrictions of a closed economy and pushed opening it up. In extreme cases, some even believe that the virus does not exists. At the same time, some members of the public view the virus as high risk and have concerns about how some people do not follow protection guidelines. The public debate persists.

Smallpox
An effective vaccine from a milder virus called cowpox was developed. The vaccine stimulated the immune system to produce antibodies against the virus.

Influenza (Asian Flu)
A vaccine was developed to slow the pandemic.

Influenza (Hong-Kong Flu)
A vaccine was developed.

Ebola
Contact tracing was used in 20 Ebola outbreaks to successfully control Ebola.

Leprosy
Medicines were developed to treat people infected with the bacteria. The type of antibiotic treatment depends on the type of leprosy a person has, tuberculoid (mild), lepromatous (severe), or borderline (both tuberculoid and lepromatous).

Fast Facts
Although some past pandemics ended, the viruses or bacteria that caused them still returned years later.

•

Some diseases such as malaria, measles, tuberculosis, and leprosy have been with humans for thousands of years with no end in sight.

HIV/AIDS
The virus became an endemic and never went away. People have learned to live with the virus using medicines to control it.

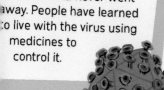

Cholera
Public health improvements, like adequate sewage and access to clean drinking water, stopped the bacteria from spreading. Even though cholera still surfaces in underdeveloped countries, it can now be treated with oral rehydration solution or intravenous fluids.

Effects of SARS-CoV-2 and the COVID-19 pandemic

We are facing a pandemic that is creating suffering, death, and upending people's lives. The effects of SARS-CoV-2 and COVID-19 stretches from health effects to social and economic effects.

stock market surges

fluctuations in job loss

supply chain disruptions

Economic Effects

The economic damage caused by SARS-CoV-2 and the COVID-19 pandemic is wide ranging. Economists focus on the virus biology and the way governments, businesses, and consumers respond to it.

consumers buying fewer things

business closings in specific industry sectors like restaurants and hospitality

uncertainty about the virus and the damage it might cause

Health Effects

We have seen how SARS CoV-2 can affect a person's physical health by infecting the respiratory and other body systems and organs. The infection may cause COVID-19, which in turn may cause more physical damage.

SARS-CoV-2, the COVID-19 pandemic, and public health measures can also affect a person's mental health. Surveys show a major increase in the number of adults who report symptoms of stress, anxiety, fear, sadness, depression, and loneliness compared to before the pandemic. However, mental health is still under-researched. The larger effects of SARS-CoV-2 and the COVID-19 pandemic on mental health still remains unclear.

Education

Changes to in-person education with online education have been affecting children and young people, creating mental and physical challenges like changing sleeping patterns. Students from the less privileged backgrounds have experienced larger negative impacts due to limited access to digital resources, and the high cost of internet connectivity.

indigenous
peoples

young people

persons with
disabilities

older persons

those living
in poverty

Social Effects

SARS-CoV-2 and the COVID-19 pandemic affects all parts of the population. It is especially damaging to social groups that are most vulnerable.

A pandemic might bring out the best or worst in people. Some will rise to help others in need. However, fear and anxiety about SARS-CoV-2 and COVID-19 might cause some to bully, mistreat, intimidate, discriminate, avoid, or reject others, even if a person might not have the virus. Showing respect to others will help people unite.

Some social research show that health and economic effects impact poor people more than other groups. For example, migrants, refugees, or displaced persons may experience fewer employment opportunities or increased negative emotions from others. If social issues are left unattended, there may be increased inequality, exclusion, discrimination, and unemployment.

Environmental Effects

SARS-CoV-2 and the COVID-19 pandemic urgency has brought light to global environmental concerns. Environmental and climate factors like temperature and humidity, increased wind speeds and greater ultraviolet (UV) light index, poor air quality, and extreme climate and weather mold the environment for SARS-CoV-2 to thrive globally.

But there are also effects from pandemic lockdown.

Negative effects
Global health
Economy
Reduction in waste recycling
PPE pollution

Positive effects
Clean beaches
Decline in air pollution
Decline in nitrogen dioxide (NO_2) concentration
Reduction of environmental noise level

All these factors pose risks that ultimately influence public health response to protect people.

Broadening Gaps

SARS-CoV-2 and the COVID-19 pandemic broadens the gaps for health, social, economic, and environmental effects in rates of infection, illness, and death. This is particularly true for racial and ethnic minority groups. Inequities like discrimination; occupation; educational, income, and wealth gaps; healthcare access and utilization; and housing put people at risk of becoming sick and dying from COVID-19. If the pandemic persists, COVID-19 cases and hospitalizations in communities with racial and ethnic minority groups may increase. Even public health measures intended to protect people may cause harm like lost jobs, limited access to services, and increased stress.

Government, SARS-CoV-2, and the COVID-19 pandemic

A pandemic can last months on end and affect numerous people, communities, the nation, and the world. Overcoming a pandemic requires coordinating all departments of government locally and nationally as well as working with partners globally to address many issues. Governments must respond to the needs of people, health and medical issues, critical infrastructure, private sector activities, movement of goods and activities, and economic and security considerations.

Truth, Trust, and Transparent Communication

People need clear, factual, scientifically accurate information about SARS-CoV-2, COVID-19, tests, vaccines, and other related issues. Being truthful and transparent builds trust with the public, leaders, and decisions makers, and keeps everyone informed and engaged about the current state of the pandemic.

Manage Testing, Vaccines, Medicines, and Medical Materials

The public needs safe, effective tests, vaccines, medicines, and medical materials. Managing the upstream development and production and downstream distribution of all materials, and ensuring they get to all people in a timely manner, in as many locations as possible, increases the chances of saving lives and decreasing the spread of the pandemic.

Advance Scientific Knowledge

The world needs continued scientific research on new vaccines and medicines to defend against the pandemic. Activities like understanding the virus's biology, transmission, and genetic sequencing may help scientists to innovate solutions that could protect people from new variants of the virus.

Implement Public Health Measures

To protect the public from the health effects when there are high levels of virus transmission, governments may use the best scientific public health measures learned from experiences with past epidemics and pandemics. The use of a few or all public health measures may vary by virus transmission rates in each location.

Examples of public health measures: universal face mask use, physical distancing, testing, avoiding unnecessary indoor spaces, identifying and isolating cases, protecting high-risk groups, protecting healthcare and essential workers, postponing travel, enhancing ventilation in closed spaces, hand washing, vaccinating widely, conducting contact tracing, and reducing contact with others through a "lockdown" or "quarantine."

Expand Economic Relief

Economically, governments distribute loans and grant monies to individuals and businesses to soften the hardship caused by the pandemic.

Government Response Outcomes

When implemented together, government actions can reduce virus transmission; reduce long-term disability and death; and limit the pandemic's damage to the economy. They can also improve health fairness, help manage hospital bed space, safely reopen schools, and keep essential businesses operating. If everyone were to follow these best practices, it could help communities move toward a safe return to everyday activities.

Partner with Global Leaders

Collaborate and share data with the international community to combat SARS-CoV-2 and COVID-19 and prepare for future pandemics.

What public health practices have you seen in your community?

You might notice that schools, some offices and stores, and restaurants might close...and sports games might get cancelled. People may be encouraged not to leave their homes.
Some people may even prepare by buying supplies like food, water, cleaning products, and other items to get through the time at home during the pandemic.

Pandemic Severity Index

Projected number of deaths

Projected number of deaths	Pandemic Severity Index
>1,800,000	5
900,000 - <1,800,000	4
450,000 - <900,000	3
90,000 - <450,000	2
<90,000	1

COMBATTING CORONAVIRUS

Ongoing Research

Scientists worldwide pivot their research to SARS-CoV-2. Some are studying how SARS-CoV-2 spreads and how it infects humans. Some are also looking at the differences between this new coronavirus and other viruses. Many are now spending their days conducting research that touches all facets of how SARS-CoV-2 and COVID-19 affect our lives.

Developing Tests

With a coronavirus pandemic, developing and deploying testing for SARS-CoV-2 is crucial. Without test, no one knows who has been infected unless a person shows COVID-19 symptoms. It becomes even more difficult since more than half of the people infected do not show any signs or symptoms of being infected. Labs and companies around the world continue to develop tests.

What are scientist doing about SARS-CoV-2 and COVID-19?

Because SARS-CoV-2 is a new coronavirus that has never been seen before, scientists around the world are constantly learning new things about it. By studying it, they can find ways to reduce its spread and better understand how to keep people safe and healthy.

Medicines and Treatments

Some scientists are working on treatments using antibodies from recovered COVID-19 patients. They are also testing existing medicines to see if any might be effective. There is ongoing collaboration to manufacture medicines and ensure the public has access to them.

Developing Vaccines

Scientists have been successful in developing vaccines in record time. But they did not start from scratch. Past research on SARS, MERS, and influenza has helped along with technological advancements. Now, there are several promising vaccines in large-scale studies that may offer long term protection. Scientists closely monitor new vaccine safety and efficacy. At the same time, governments also monitor safety and help to fast-track the process.

77

Medicines and treatments for COVID-19

Scientists around the world are investigating new and existing medicines for COVID-19. Medicines are remedies and drugs that people take to treat a disease or illness. Medicines that minimize the duration and impact of COVID-19 in people can potentially reduce the number of people checking into hospitals.

Existing Medicines

Scientists are testing medicines that work for other diseases to find out if they might benefit people who develop COVID-19. Some of these medicines include steroids or antibiotics.

Antibiotics are used in patients with bacterial infections like pneumonia. Researchers are also investigating specific antibiotics as a potential anti-inflammatory treatment.

Steroids are drugs used to reduce inflammation. Certain commonly available steroids are often used by doctors to tamp down the body's immune system, alleviating inflammation, swelling, and pain. In severely affected patients, low-dose steroids may help calm a hyperactive immune system from destroying cells or damaging organs.

But no treatment comes without **risk.** Steroids can have side effects like increased risk of bacterial or fungal infections, high blood sugar, muscle weakness, and digestive system bleeding. They may also do more harm than good in patients with milder cases of COVID-19. Antibiotics use may cause antibiotic-resistant bacteria.

COVID-19

Monoclonal Antibodies

Monoclonal Antibody Therapy (Emergency Use/Unapproved Product)

Monoclonal antibodies are laboratory-made proteins that act like antibodies to fight off harmful antigens. This investigational therapy uses monoclonal antibodies to bind specifically to certain cells or proteins. The treatment's goal is to stimulate the patient's immune system to attack those cells. This treatment may be used as a preventative measure while waiting for a vaccine to take effect.

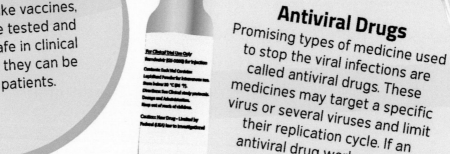

New Medicines
Developing new medicines takes time. Like vaccines, they must be tested and confirmed safe in clinical trials before they can be given to patients.

Antiviral Drugs
Promising types of medicine used to stop the viral infections are called antiviral drugs. These medicines may target a specific virus or several viruses and limit their replication cycle. If an antiviral drug works against a virus, it can help control the spread of that virus.

COVID-19
Convalescent Plasma Therapy
(Emergency Use/Unapproved Product)
This therapy takes some blood that has antibodies (plasma) from recovered COVID-19 patients and put it into a sick patient's body. This treatment hopes to stimulate the sick patient's immune system to begin destroying the virus.

Evidence suggests that benefit is most likely in patients treated in the early stage of infection. But it has little or no effect on mortality when used in late-stage hospitalized patients. This therapy may also have no effects on variants. This type of therapy has been used on SARS, MERS, and the H1N1 flu. It dates back as far as the 1918 flu pandemic.

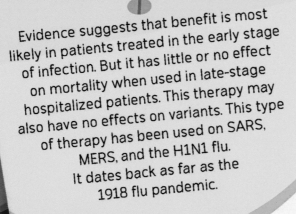

Blood Plasma

White Blood Cells and Platelets

Red Blood Cells

Other Treatments Options
There are medicines that can be used to treat COVID-19 symptoms such as fever, body aches, and nasal congestion caused by SARS-CoV-2. If symptoms are severe, a doctor may provide medication to reduce fever, supplemental oxygen, pain medication, or fluids to reduce the chances of dehydration.

The use of stem cells are another emerging potential therapy in treating COVID-19.

An Ideal Scenario
The ideal scenario to control a viral infection is to find an antiviral drug for those who were infected and to have a safe vaccine to help prevent infection.

Fast Facts
Antibiotics are ineffective against COVID-19 because this illness is a viral infection. Antibiotics are only effective on bacterial infections.

Vaccines

Vaccines are considered the most promising tool to slow down the pandemic. As a result, their development, testing, and monitoring are critical worldwide.

What Is a Vaccine?

Vaccines are biological preparations that are used to make people immune to certain diseases. The biological agent is usually the whole or part of the live, inactivated, or synthetic bacteria or virus.

Traditional Vaccines

Types of Vaccines

Scientists take many approaches to design vaccines. The nature of the virus, the infection, and other considerations determine which approach scientists will take to create a vaccine.

Live, attenuated vaccine

This vaccine uses a weakened (attenuated) form of the virus. Because this vaccine infection is similar to the natural infection, it has a strong, long-lasting immune response.

Subunit vaccine

This vaccine uses parts of the virus (like the protein) instead of the entire virus. Because it uses specific virus parts, this vaccine has very strong immune response.

Inactivated vaccine

This vaccine uses a dead (inactivated) version of the virus. Inactivation results from heat, chemicals, or radiation. This vaccine provides less protection and strength than live, attenuated vaccines.

Toxoid vaccine

This vaccine uses the toxins part of the pathogen (virus, bacterium, or fungus) to generate a vaccine. The toxins are purified and weakened so they cannot cause illness. In this state, they are called toxoids. As a vaccine, injected toxoid generates antibodies, which bind with toxins to neutralize its effects.

Bacteria emitting toxin

Toxin

Modified Toxoid

Experimental Vaccines

Messenger RNA (mRNA) vaccine

This newer type of vaccine uses part of the virus's own genetic material to stimulate an immune response.

With mRNA vaccines, rather than a cell's nucleus transcribing (copying) a virus's DNA or RNA to make mRNA, scientists genetically engineer mRNA in a lab.

When injected into a person's body, the lab-made mRNA bypasses the cell's nucleus and binds directly to the cell's ribosomes, which translate (decode) it to make the desired harmless virus proteins. The body's immune system responds to the foreign proteins by producing antibodies to protect cells.

Like other mRNA, the lab-made mRNA is short-lived and rapidly broken down after it has done its job.

Scientists believe the similar to natural immune response that mRNA vaccines induce would be very efficient. It would also be stable, inexpensive, and easy to make.

Viral vector vaccine

Viral vector vaccines use recombinant DNA technology—a process of creating DNA molecules in a lab by combining a piece of one DNA from one species with a piece of DNA from another species (recombinant) to form a new strand of DNA. This is sometimes referred to as "chimera" or "genetic engineering."

For example, the genetic material from a virus is placed in a modified version of a different virus like adenovirus (viral vector) to carry the DNA or RNA to the cell's nucleus where it is transcribed (copied) and made into mRNA.

The mRNA moves to the cell's cytoplasm and binds directly to the cell's ribosomes, which translate (decode) it to make the desired harmless virus proteins. The body's immune system responds to the foreign proteins by producing antibodies to protect cells.

What's in a Vaccine?

Water
Main ingredient.

Adjuvants
Work to boost the immune response.
Example: Aluminum

Active ingredient
Small harmless virus or bacteria particle (antigen) the body immunizes against.
Examples: DNA/RNA, protein, or killed or weakened virus.

Preservatives
Allow the vaccine to be stored in vials for quality and safety.
Example: Sorbitol

Residual traces
Manufacturing particles that make it into the vaccine.
Example: Formaldehyde

Fast Facts
Vaccines may last for the short or long term depending on the type.

Common Concerns with Vaccines

Historically, there is ample scientific research that vaccines are more beneficial than the risks associated with them. Even so, many still have concerns.

● A vaccine aims to generate antibodies, and sometimes it may not work as expected in everyone or in all cases.

● Live, attenuated vaccines may cause sickness in people with weakened immune systems. These vaccines need continuous refrigeration so the weakened virus does not lose its biological properties.

● Inactivated vaccines may not be as accurate in imitating the virus as a live attenuated vaccine. They often require more than one dose and "booster shots" to build immunity.

● Identifying the best antigen and separating it from the virus may not always be possible with subunit vaccines.

● Highly variable reactions in some vaccines from "adjuvants" used to help create and intensify an early, high, and long-lasting immune response.

● Uncertainty that clinical trials test a large enough group of people to evaluate safety for a drug that would be administered to so many.

● When a vaccine worsens illness instead of protecting from the disease, this phenomenon is called antibody-dependent enhancement (ADE).

● Questions arise about efficacy surrounding potential vaccines from clinical trials.

● Some people may be allergic to a vaccine because of its ingredients. People who have a history of severe allergic reactions should talk to their healthcare provider for guidance before getting vaccinated.

● Sometimes a vaccine might not be as efficient in suppressing the virus as scientists hope. In this case, medicines such as antiviral drugs are needed to take care of virus suppression.

83

Vaccines and stages of development

Vaccines go through several stages after discovery, including animal trials, human trials, regulatory approval, and finally manufacturing.

Several hundred volunteers

Phase II Testing:
Objectives

Expand safety testing

Identify most common short-term side effects

Measure the body's immune response

Watch for signs of protection from vaccine

Study halts if severe reaction occurs **!**

SARS-CoV-2 Vaccines **6 months**	Traditional Vaccines **32 months**

20-100 volunteers

Phase I Clinical Trials:
Objectives

Test safety

Identify side effects

Understand how vaccine does relate to side effects

Observe if vaccine causes an immune response

Study halts if severe reaction occurs **!**

SARS-CoV-2 Vaccines **6 months**	Traditional Vaccines **30 months**

Exploratory research:

The vaccine candidate is found to prompt the human immune system to generate antibodies so it can go into development.

Pre-clinical studies:

The new vaccine candidate is tested first in immune cell culture and then in small animals (often mice) that have been modified with the human ACE2 gene. The vaccine must cause an immune response to move to the next stage of testing. Toxicity studies are done in animals to check for safety concerns.

SARS-CoV-2 Vaccines **0 months**	Traditional Vaccines **18-30 months**

How were SARS-CoV-2 Vaccines Developed So Fast?

Rapid turnaround of the SARS-CoV-2 vaccine was less than eight months. This was achieved by:

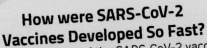

Knowledge from similar coronaviruses and influenzas.

Funding from government and private sources

Crunching timelines overlapping "phase 1 and II" and "phase II and III

Newer mRNA technology

Keen volunteers

Priority and collaboration

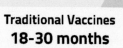

1000 or more volunteers

Phase III:
Objectives

Expand safety testing

Identify how disease rates compare between people who get the vaccine and those who do not

Understand how well the vaccine protects people from disease

Study halts if severe reaction occurs **!**

If successful, the vaccine maker applies to regulatory authorities for a license to market the vaccine

Government approves the vaccine ONLY if it is safe and effective and the benefits outweigh the risks

SARS-CoV-2 Vaccines
0 months

Traditional Vaccines
30 months

Emergency Use:
In a pandemic, the government may grant emergency use of the vaccine. The vaccine then goes to manufacture. If the vaccine continues to be effective, the vaccine maker may apply for approval and license.

Phase IV Treatment is Approved:

Vaccine goes to manufacturing and into arms

Government closely monitors the vaccine's safety after the public begins using it

Researchers continue to collect data on the vaccine's long-term benefit and side effects

Fast Facts

In Phase I of the SARS-CoV-2 vaccine, non-human primates were vaccinated with wild-type SARS-CoV-2 to understand if the vaccine might enhance the disease. Studies to date did not find evidence associated with enhanced disease.

The government sets rules for the three phases of clinical trials to ensure safety.

Some governments have a national monitoring program to collect and review reports of any health problems that develop after a person gets a vaccine. Anyone can submit a report.

Medical recommendations may change if safety concerns arise.

Manufacture of the Vaccine:

Large-scale manufacture goes ahead! Quality control and post-marketing surveillance are used to find rare adverse effects

Government inspects manufacturer facility regularly for quality and safety

Vaccines are made in batches called lots.

Manufacturer tests all lots for safety, purity, and potency

Lots are released after government reviews for safety

SARS-CoV-2 Vaccines
6 months

Traditional Vaccines
12-24 months

Vaccines and major milestones

1796

A Vaccine Helped Eliminate Smallpox Viral Disease

Vaccination with vaccinia virus has been directly responsible for the successful eradication of smallpox.

What Is Smallpox?
Smallpox was one of the most infectious and deadly diseases in the world caused by the variola virus. It afflicted millions of people. Scientists estimate that smallpox was responsible for 300–500 million deaths during the 20th century.

Smallpox virus

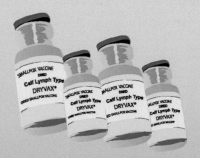

Dairymaids Help Create Vaccine
An English doctor, Edward Jenner, observed that milkmaids who had gotten cowpox did not show any symptoms of smallpox after variolation. Variolation, or inoculation, meant taking material from smallpox sores and giving it to people who had never had smallpox.

Vaccine Inoculation Creates Immunity
After his observation that cowpox infection seemed to protect humans against smallpox, Jenner extracted the cowpox matter from a blister on the hand of an English milkmaid and inoculated an 8-year-old boy—the boy had mild illness and recovered. He then inoculated the boy with smallpox matter and the boy did not develop smallpox. Jenner had demonstrated smallpox immunization.

1885

The First Vaccine Protects Against Rabies

Vaccination with rabies virus weakened in rabbits and harvested from their spinal cords for the successful treatment of rabies.

What Is Rabies?
Rabies is a viral disease that causes inflammation of the brain and is transmitted through the bite of an animal. It has almost 100% mortality rate.

Pasteur Develops Vaccine for Rabies
After years of successful tests treating chicken cholera and anthrax bacteria, Louis Pasteur turned to rabies. He grew the virus in rabbits' spinal cord and weakened it by drying the infected nerve tissue. He tested the vaccine in 50 dogs before testing it in humans.

Vaccine Inoculation Successfully Treats Rabies
Pasteur used the vaccine on a young boy named Joseph Meister who was severely bitten by a rabid dog. Pasteur gave Meister 13 inoculations of the weakened virus. After three months, Pasteur examined the boy and found that he was in good health. Later, over 350+ people were treated successfully.

Other vaccines developed with this method include influenza vaccine (1940s), polio vaccine (1950s), and hepatitis A vaccine (1991).

1937

The First Vaccine Protects Against Yellow Fever

What Is Yellow Fever?
Yellow fever is a deadly flu-like disease spread by A. aegypti mosquitoes.

Max Theiler Develops Vaccine for Yellow Fever
Following years of yellow fever research, Theiler discovered that if the yellow fever virus had continuous passage in mice, its strength diminished for rhesus monkeys. He then found that a monkey that recovered from a fever after injection with yellow fever passed multiple times in mice became immune. Eventually, he modified the virus to an exceedingly low virulence to create the 17D virus strain.

Vaccine 17D Inoculation Immunizes against Yellow Fever
From 1940 to 1947, twenty-eight million doses of the 17D vaccine was produced and eliminated yellow fever as a major disease.

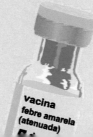

vacina
febre amarela
(atenuada)

1979

The First Recombinant DNA Technology Protects Against Hepatitis B

Control over genetic material enables scientists to produce a new generation of vaccines that improve health, cost, and production.

What Is Hepatitis B?
Hepatitis B is a serious liver infection caused by the hepatitis B virus. It is the most common liver infection in the world.

Paul Berg Creates First Recombinant DNA Molecules
In 1972, Berg took DNA from the SV40 monkey virus and spliced it into DNA cut from a bacterial virus known as the lambda bacteriophage. The result led to the virus replicating inside cells, with the expression of bacteriophage genes. Berg's research paved the way for other scientists.

Paul Berg wrote about the potential dangers of recombinant DNA research. Later, the National Institutes of Health produced a document entitled "Guidelines for Research Involving Recombinant DNA Molecules" that cover responsibilities, safety, and other topics involving research with this technology.

Hepatitis B Subunit Vaccine That Prevents Hepatitis B
In 1981, William Rutter, Pablo Valenzuela, and colleagues developed the recombinant vaccine by taking the hepatitis B surface antigen DNA and inserting it into yeast (free of any human blood products) to produce only noninfectious surface protein, eliminating the infectious viral DNA. This vaccine is still in use today.

Vaccines and SARS-CoV-2

Scientists are working very hard to develop vaccines for SARS-CoV-2 to prevent new infections.

Lessons from SARS-CoV and MERS-CoV

Vaccine development from SARS-CoV and MERS-CoV paved the way for expedited development of SARS-CoV-2 vaccines. Pre-clinical studies were completed with SARS-CoV and MERS-CoV vaccines and evaluated in small human trials. But, development waned when the viruses faded. Some things that scientists learned:

Animal studies had concerns about enhanced disease with vaccines, but none was seen in human studies.

Some research supported the theory that vaccination had the potential to prevent SARS-CoV-2 infection.

Both vaccines targeted the spike protein of each virus and this became the major target for the SARS-CoV-2 vaccine development.

Vaccines Approaches for SARS-CoV-2

Most, if not all, vaccine types are being used by different companies to develop SARS-CoV-2 vaccines. Some take the traditional approach like an inactivated virus or live attenuated virus. Others work with a newer approach like recombinant proteins and vectors. Some, like DNA and RNA, were never used in a vaccine before.

Why Do We Need One or More Vaccine Doses?

Vaccine development takes many variables into account like the type of virus, how the immune system responds to the virus, and what parts of the virus can be used to generate an immune response. Because of this complexity, sometimes a person may require more than one dose. Here are some reasons for more than one dose.

To have more complete immunity than the first dose offered.

To protect the person if the first dose had no effect.

To have a longer-lasting immune response if the first wears off.

To develop the best immune response to ensure everyone is protected.

To protect from new mutations of a virus.

Herd Immunity by Vaccine

Vaccines have the potential to protect the entire population. With a vaccine the world might be able to achieve immunity and herd immunity safely.

The idea is that if 75 percent or more people get vaccinated and develop immunity, outbreaks become so low that people who do not have immunity benefit. The virus has fewer people to infect and eventually dies out.

The opposite is also true. If too few people get vaccinated, the population would be at risk of outbreaks or ongoing pandemic the more the virus spreads.

!

Vaccine and Variants

So far, studies show that antibodies stimulated by currently authorized vaccines are a little less effective on new variants, but are still producing enough immunity to protect from those new variants. Scientists continue to analyze vaccination data to understand the vaccines effectiveness. They are also reviewing the data to understand if vaccines may need reformulating to address new variants, which may indicate that yearly shots may be needed to protect against new variants. Studies are ongoing.

Fast Facts

For coronavirus, recombinant vector vaccines use adenoviruses a type of common cold virus) to carry the genetic instructions into the host cell.

●

It is unclear whether SARS-CoV-2 vaccine protection from a single dose would be long-lasting, or how long antibodies would last after getting second dose.

●

People taking the second dose of SARS-CoV-2 vaccine have reported experiencing stronger illness like low-grade fever, or pain and redness than the first dose.

●

The flu vaccine helps the body to develop its own defenses against the flu. But, because influenza mutates regularly, flu shots are needed every year.

●

As a precaution, some vaccine makers are developing vaccine boosters to protect against SARS-CoV-2 variants.

Some worldwide vaccines in use for SARS-CoV-2

!

Vaccines may be less effective against emerging virus variants, but may continue to be effective against preventing severe illness.

Several vaccines have become available for use against SARS-CoV-2.

Pfizer-Biontech

Vaccine Type: mRNA vaccine

Emergency Use Authorization (EUA): approved in several countries.

Effectiveness: Showed to be 95% effective at preventing COVID-19 with no serious safety concerns after two doses in phase III trials.

Doses: 2
21 days apart.

Storage: Stored at ultracold temperature of -94° F (-70 °C). Special designed freezer cases with dry ice and GPS trackers.

Moderna/NIAID

Vaccine Type: mRNA vaccine

Emergency Use Authorization (EUA): approved in several countries.

Effectiveness: Showed to be 94.5% effective at preventing COVID-19 with no serious safety concerns in phase III trials.

Doses: 2
28 days apart.

Storage: Stored at -4° F (-20° C). Keeps at refrigerator temperatures for 1 month. May be accessible to areas without specialized freezers.

Oxford-AstraZeneca

Vaccine Type: Recombinant vector vaccine

Emergency Use Authorization (EUA): approved in several countries.

Effectiveness: Showed to be 62-70% effective at preventing COVID-19.

Doses: 2
8 to 12 weeks apart.

Storage: Stored at normal refrigeration temperatures for at least 6 months.

Cansino-Beijing

Vaccine Type: Weakened adenovirus that naturally infects humans

Emergency Use Authorization (EUA): Approved by China's military.

Effectiveness: Ongoing trials. Efficacy not yet known.

Doses: 1

Storage: 2-8° C

Coronavac by Sinovac vaccine

Vaccine Type: Inactivated version of SARS-CoV-2

Emergency Use Authorization (EUA): Approved in China.

Effectiveness: Estimates vary on effectiveness ranging from 50.5% to 78%.

Doses: 2
14 days apart.

Storage: 2-8° C

Bharat Biotech Covaxin

Vaccine Type: Inactivated whole SARS-CoV-2

Emergency Use Authorization (EUA): approved in several countries.

Effectiveness: Interim trials show 81% effective.

Doses: 2
28 days apart.

Storage: Can be stored at refrigerator temperature.

Johnson & Johnson /Janssen

Vaccine Type: Recombinant vector vaccine

Emergency Use Authorization (EUA): approved in several countries.

Effectiveness: Showed to be 72% effective at preventing COVID-19 in the U.S. (64% effective in South Africa due to the B.1.351 variant).

Showed 66% effective overall at preventing moderate to severe COVID-19 in the U.S. (82% effective in South Africa due to the B.1.351 variant).

Demonstrated 85% effectiveness overall protection against COVID-19 hospitalization as of day 28 after vaccination.

Doses: 1

Storage: Can be stored for months at normal refrigerator temperatures.

Sinopharm (Beijing Institute of Biological Products) BBIBP-CorV

Vaccine Type: Inactivated modified SARS-CoV-2 that cannot replicate

Emergency Use Authorization (EUA): approved in several countries.

Effectiveness: Showed to be more than 79% effective from late-stage trials.

The data has not been published.

Doses: 2
21 days apart.

Storage: 2-8° C

Sinopharm (Wuhan Institute of Biological Products)

Vaccine Type: Inactivated modified SARS-CoV-2 that cannot replicate

Emergency Use Authorization (EUA): approved in several countries.

Effectiveness: Little is known about its efficacy.

Doses: 2
21 days apart.

Storage: 2-8° C

Sputnik V by Gamaleya Research Institute

Vaccine Type: Weakened adenoviruses, modified to not replicate in humans; coded for the SARS-CoV-2 spike protein.

Emergency Use Authorization (EUA): approved in several countries.

Effectiveness: Estimated at 91.4% effective from trials.

Doses: 2
21 days apart.

Storage: -18° C (frozen) and 2-8° C (Lyophilised)

Vector Institute vaccine

Vaccine Type: Coronavirus peptides

Emergency Use Authorization (EUA): Approved in Russia

Effectiveness: Little is known about its efficacy.

Doses: 2
21 days apart.

Storage: 2-8° C

Fast Facts

Some scientists are developing next-generation nasal spray and pill vaccines.

Other Vaccine Candidates in the Pipeline

There are many other vaccines being researched. More than 40 candidate vaccines are in human trials, while over 150 were in pre-clinical trials.

91

92

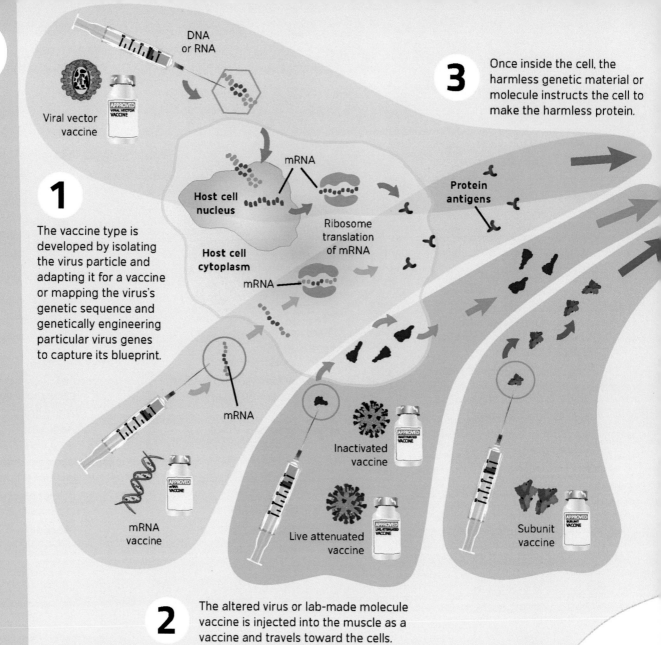

Viral vector vaccine

DNA or RNA

APPROVED VIRAL VECTOR VACCINE

3 Once inside the cell, the harmless genetic material or molecule instructs the cell to make the harmless protein.

mRNA

Host cell nucleus

Host cell cytoplasm

mRNA

Ribosome translation of mRNA

Protein antigens

1 The vaccine type is developed by isolating the virus particle and adapting it for a vaccine or mapping the virus's genetic sequence and genetically engineering particular virus genes to capture its blueprint.

mRNA

mRNA vaccine

APPROVED mRNA VACCINE

Inactivated vaccine

APPROVED INACTIVATED VACCINE

Live attenuated vaccine

APPROVED LIVE ATTENUATED VACCINE

Subunit vaccine

APPROVED SUBUNIT VACCINE

2 The altered virus or lab-made molecule vaccine is injected into the muscle as a vaccine and travels toward the cells.

How do vaccines work?

Vaccines help teach the body to fight the virus by imitating an infection. They do this by safely stimulating the body to create antibodies that fight an infection the first time it is encountered. At the same time, the vaccine stimulation causes the immune system to produce a set of T-lymphocytes and B-lymphocytes that remember how to fight the same infection in the future.

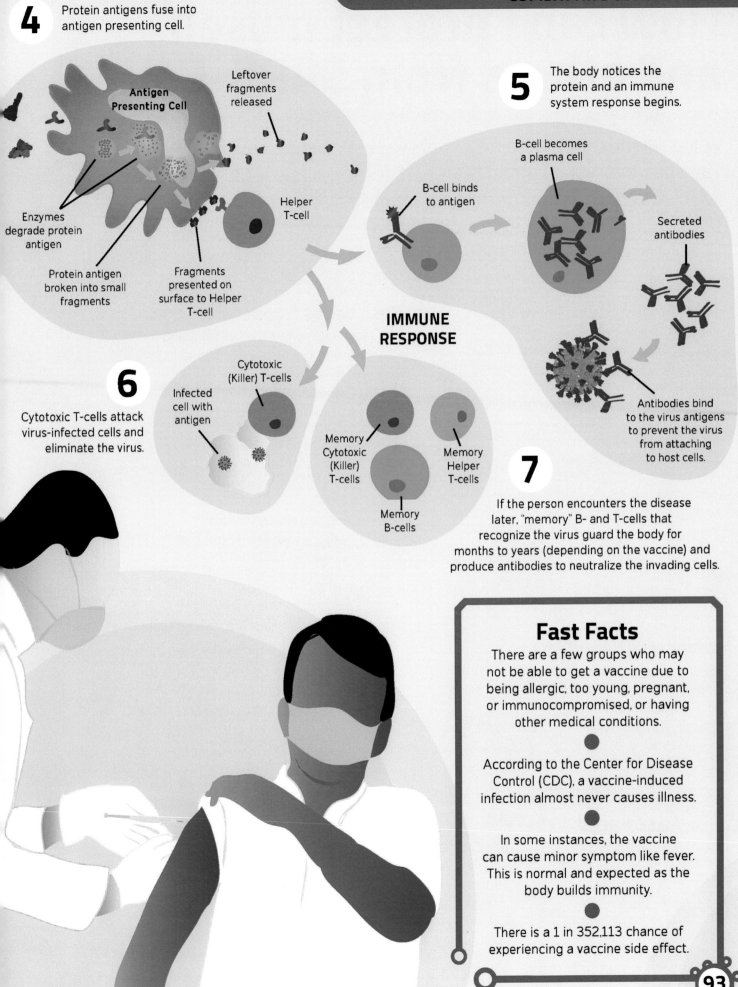

4 Protein antigens fuse into antigen presenting cell.

Antigen Presenting Cell

Leftover fragments released

Helper T-cell

Enzymes degrade protein antigen

Protein antigen broken into small fragments

Fragments presented on surface to Helper T-cell

5 The body notices the protein and an immune system response begins.

B-cell becomes a plasma cell

B-cell binds to antigen

Secreted antibodies

Antibodies bind to the virus antigens to prevent the virus from attaching to host cells.

IMMUNE RESPONSE

6 Cytotoxic T-cells attack virus-infected cells and eliminate the virus.

Infected cell with antigen

Cytotoxic (Killer) T-cells

Memory Cytotoxic (Killer) T-cells

Memory B-cells

Memory Helper T-cells

7 If the person encounters the disease later, "memory" B- and T-cells that recognize the virus guard the body for months to years (depending on the vaccine) and produce antibodies to neutralize the invading cells.

Fast Facts

There are a few groups who may not be able to get a vaccine due to being allergic, too young, pregnant, or immunocompromised, or having other medical conditions.

According to the Center for Disease Control (CDC), a vaccine-induced infection almost never causes illness.

In some instances, the vaccine can cause minor symptom like fever. This is normal and expected as the body builds immunity.

There is a 1 in 352,113 chance of experiencing a vaccine side effect.

How can I protect myself and others from SARS-CoV-2?

While scientists develop and improve tests, medicines, and vaccines, everyone can do their part to stop or slow the spread of SARS-CoV-2 by either getting vaccinated or doing some familiar, but simple things. It is also a good idea to continue practicing these activities even if a person has gotten a vaccine.

Quarantine (if necessary)

If a person has been exposed to SARS-CoV-2, they should quarantine at home for 14 days after their last contact with a person infected with SARS-CoV-2. Watch for fever, cough, shortness of breath, or other COVID-19 symptoms. If possible, avoid others, especially higher risk individuals.

Wash hands frequently

This is especially important after going to the bathroom, before eating, after coughing or sneezing, after playing with animals, and after going outside. Because SARS-CoV-2 has a lipid shell, it can be deactivated using soap. Wash hands with soap and water or use an alcohol-based hand sanitizer if soap and water are unavailable.

Keep your hands away from your face

That means, no nose picking, thumb sucking, or touching your eyes, nose, or mouth.

Good handwashing (and hand sanitization) tips:

Use soapy water to kill viruses by making them explode.

Scrub for more than 20 seconds (sing "Happy Birthday" twice).

Wash front and back, and scrub between fingers and thumbs.

Scrub your hands before you put them under the water.

Dry your hands well.

Cover coughs and sneezes

If someone gets the coughs and sneezes, they can cough or sneeze into a tissue and discard it in a closed bin. They can even catch the particles in the bend of their elbow!

Fast Facts

Wearing a mask may cause dry skin, bruising, redness, and inflammation. Follow a gentle skin care routine to protect your skin.

Practice physical distancing

Scientists and doctors say it might be possible to be infected if someone is within 6 feet of another person. Therefore, it is especially important for people to stay a safe distance of 6 feet or more away from others.

Avoid crowds

Plan ahead. Perform activities online. If a person must perform a necessary activity, do so when the location is less crowded. What are other ways you can think of?

Wear a mask or cloth face covering

This protects you from infected people and protects other people if you are infected. A mask is a physical barrier that helps block splashes and large droplets that may contain viral particles from reaching your nose and mouth. In some cases, a mask might also have an attached plastic shield to protect your eyes. Doubling and tripling up on surgical or homemade masks may provide better protection. The key is a tight fit with no gaps.

There are several types of masks. These are some of the most common:

N95 respirator

N95 respirator is a respiratory protective device designed to achieve a very close facial fit and very efficient filtration of airborne particles. However, the CDC does not recommend this mask for the general public because they are considered critical supplies for healthcare workers and medical first responders. Requires a simple fit test to determine if the mask is a good fit.

KN95 mask

A KN95 mask is a respiratory protective mask designed to achieve a close facial fit. KN95s is rated to capture 95% of particles. Requires a simple fit test to determine if the mask is a good fit.

Surgical mask

Surgical masks are used by healthcare providers and now it is recommended to the general public. These are an affordable and simple tool to decrease the spread of the virus. They provide a good physical barrier against large droplets containing viral particles. However, they do not provide complete protection because of the loose fit between the surface of the mask and your face. There is potential for droplet nuclei lower than 5 microns to pass through the mask fibers, and this type of masks may not protect you with one layer

Homemade face coverings

Homemade face coverings will not completely protect you against infectious diseases because they also have a loose fit. The material that these are made from is not as good a barrier as surgical masks. However, wearing a mask made with two layers or more, combined with social distancing (keeping at least 6 feet apart from others), can be effective.

Did you know that 70% alcohol (ethanol/isopropyl) solution is more efficient in inactivating enveloped viral particles than 100% ethanol?

A solution of 70% ethanol contains 30% water. This is the ideal ratio for killing bacteria and inactivating enveloped viruses. The 70% alcohol solution breaks down the lipid layer of the virus envelope. This stops its ability to infect cells. Viruses might be killed by 80% to 90% alcohol solutions, but these are not as efficient as a 70% alcohol solution. Never use 100% alcohol, because at this concentration, the evaporation rate is too fast. It is inefficient to completely inactivate enveloped viruses or to kill bacteria.

Wear an eye covering or face shield

Recommendations have been made by health officials to also wear protective eye coverings to prevent virus entry through the eyes since they are rich in ACE2 receptors and TMPRSS2 entry facilitators. Eye protection may be plastic face shields or eyewear that fully covers the eyes, blocking any particles from entering.

Clean surfaces regularly

This includes food packages bought from the grocery store.

Supply shortage for items to protect from the virus or for normal home use.

Health of family and friends.

Getting the virus and getting sick.

Watch out for COVID-19 fatigue!
COVID-19 fatigue and/or burnout is when a person has reached their capacity to cope and experiences various mental, emotional, and physical symptoms from constant exposure to pandemic stressors like social distancing, isolation from family/friends, fears of contracting SARS-CoV-2 and developing COVID-19, numerous virtual meetings, grief, financial stress, and more.

Are You Feeling a Mix of Emotions during Coronavirus?
The pandemic has caused winding emotions like avoidance, fear, and acceptance. This is normal. Some reasons why someone might experience negative emotions include:

Not being able to visit family or friends in person.

Passing the virus to others (especially those who are high risk).

Taking care of family.

Financial stress.

Worry that things— like going to the grocery store—are not safe.

Mind your mental health

SARS-CoV-2 and health measures to prevent its spread have disrupted all our lives. They can cause uncertainty, financial pressures, changed routines, and social separation. The impact can affect our mental health, including our emotional and psychological well-being. Even when the pandemic outlook improves, recognizing psychological distress like depression and stress is key to managing mental health.

Experiencing psychological distress every day can affect one's health. For example, chronic stress might cause increased risk of heart problems or diabetes. Or, one's immune system might become weakened, reducing the body's ability to fight various threats.

Keep your mind active: Enjoy a book or try a crossword or search word puzzle.

Recognize self-deception: Ways our mind convinces us of something that is not really true. These are habitual ways of thinking that are often inaccurate and negative. Identify and change damaging thoughts. Consider facts then reframe thoughts based on facts.

Recognize anxiety: Spot anxiety and manage it. Signs include uncontrollable worry, stomach issues, trouble focusing, increased heart rate, irritability, or changes in energy.

Practice good sleep hygiene: Keep a regular sleep routine. Avoid computer screens in bed. Recharge the brain by sleeping 7-9 hours each night.

Talk: Talk about feelings with someone to calm any fears. Are you lonely, sad, scared, or angry? Are you anxious or stressed? Share these feelings with someone you trust.

What You Can Control

Public health measures might limit where people can go or what they can do. These are things out of one's control. What someone can control, however, is their life and activities. What can be done to strengthen mental health? With a little creativity, the possibilities can be endless.

Trauma: Recognize vicarious, social, or physical trauma and seek out support.

Create structure and routine. Manage your day and empower yourself with choice. When facing shutdowns, curfews, or other public health measures, set regularly scheduled at-home and essential tasks.

Family time: Spend some quality time with your family.

Other activities: Gardening, arts and crafts, start a journal, make a home video, cook your favorite dish, listen to music, take a class, play an instrument or board/video game, or create a visualization life board.

Grieve: Take some time to grieve if you need it.

Meditate: Practice relaxation techniques or deep breathing. Tense and relax the muscles throughout the body. Visualize a relaxing setting.

Reconnect with nature: Go outside. Go camping, hiking, or swimming.

◀ Keeping a positive outlook and learning past lessons enable one to cope better with stressful situations, which reduces the harmful health effects of stress on one's body. These actions allow one to open up to a happier future, but always be aware of potential changes..

Your physical health

During this time of change and uncertainty, it is important to practice self-care and maintain a structured schedule. There are many ways to stay healthy while SARS-CoV-2 infections fluctuate. Take some time to care for your body and your mind. Increase your immune strength so you feel your best.

Stay physically active

► Exercise as least 30 minutes each day

► Regular exercise increases energy levels and improves your immune system. It also increases happiness, maintains health, and prevents chronic diseases. Some activities include walking, dancing, jogging, skipping rope, yoga, Pilates, cycling, pushups, sit ups, squats, or jumping jacks.

► Exercising outside is good for you and can be fun to do with others, but remember to always physically distance and wear protective masks to prevent spreading the virus to others.

Hydrate

► Drink enough water throughout the day. Avoid drinks that reduce hydration.

Fight fatigue

► Alternate sitting and standing throughout the day. Take short walks around the house or up and down stairs.

Eat healthy

▶ Eat a balanced diet and snack on healthy foods. Garlic, onions, ginger, and yogurt help the good bacteria in your body.

▶ Avoid unhealthy fats or foods that are slow to digest. Try not to eat too many fried foods, meats, and processed foods that cause inflammation.

Get good quality sleep.

▶ Sleep plays a strong role in your mental and physical health. Your body, mind, and immune system need 7-9 hours of sleep each day.

▶ A lack of sleep increases stress hormones.

Practice meditation and yoga

▶ Meditate, practice yoga, or simply enjoy doing the things that make you happy.

Avoid stress

▶ Take a time out or break and de-stress by doing nothing except practicing deep breathing or listening to music.

▶ Stepping away from problems helps clear your thoughts and gain perspective.

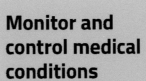

Monitor and control medical conditions

▶ Stay on top of diabetes, blood pressure, and/or other medical conditions.

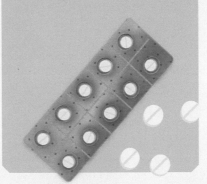

Stay connected

▶ Maintain good relationships with your loved ones.

▶ Be social—call, email, or video chat family and friends. It will reduce anxiety and stress.

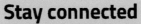

Consult your doctor

▶ Consider talking to a healthcare provider about getting vaccines, such as Influenza or SARS-CoV-2.

Life after SARS-COV-2

The introduction of SARS-CoV-2 has meant many changes to the way we live. There will continue to be economic, political, and social effects. Some things that could be changed from the way they were done before include:

Work

There might be more work-from-home opportunities. If people go into work, companies will need to have worker safety measures in place to protect and prevent the spread of the virus.

Education

Going back to school might mean a hybrid of in-class and online offerings. In-person classes may require students to wear masks and increase space between desks at least 1 meter apart so that students can learn safely.

Economic system

People may create a more shared approach to society's problems.

Manufacturing

Companies might start reviewing and revising how they create and manufacture their products globally and how they work with other countries.

Scientists Outlook

Infectious disease experts maintain that SARS-CoV-2 may never be eradicated or wiped out, but nations can bring down infections to "low levels."

New waves of infections will be determined primarily by whether or not we follow protocols, how we behave, and the decisions we make.

Service and entertainment

Service-related jobs, like retail and restaurants, and forms of live entertainment will require safety measures. They may need thoughtful innovation and creativity to accommodate new behaviors.

Pandemic

A lack of action to control the spread of the virus may mean exponential infections. Testing may be improved. Vaccines and therapeutics may help curtail infections.

Adapting to Change

With so many abrupt changes happening worldwide at the same time, people may be too stressed to take precautions. They may be too worried about the economy. They may be concerned about their and their families' health. They may want to live their normal lives, but their external environments change. They may have to change their behavior to adjust to the new way of life.

But if people fail to change and take proper precautions, they may get infected with the virus. That could result in more people getting infected with the virus. The more the virus spreads, the more safety precautions are important.

Glossary

Aerosol is small droplet nuclei that mixes with droplets in the air, which can float for long distances and cause infection after inhaling.

An **antigen** is a substance that, when introduced into the body, stimulates the production of an antibody.

Antigen Presenting Cell (APC) - a type of immune cell that boosts immune response by showing fragments of antigen on the its surface. to other immune cells. An APC is a type of phagocyte.

Antigenic refers to proteins on the virus's surface that infect the host and cause the host's immune system to respond.

Antigenic drift is the frequent and natural mutation as differences build up over time and form new virus strains.

Antigenic shift is an unexpected, large change that enables a virus strain to jump from one animal species (including humans) to another.

Capsid is a protein coat that surrounds a virus's nucleic acid.

Capsomere is a protein subunit of the capsid.

Contact tracing is when scientists identify infected people, isolate them, and then isolate the people they came in contact with.

Coronavirus [kō-rō′nă-vī′rŭs] is a genetic term that includes a large family of viruses of the Family Coronaviridae. It comes from the Latin corona, which means crown or halo.

Cytokine storms occur when the body over-produces cytokines to fight infection. This causes large scale inflammation in the body.

Droplet transmission happens when an infected person speaks, sings, coughs, or sneezes, and the droplets they produce land on a non-infected person's mouth, nose, broken skin, or eyes.

Endocytosis is the cellular process in which substances are brought into a cell.

Envelope is an enclosing outer structure formed by a double layer of phospholipid and viral proteins.

Eradication is when a virus is completely eliminated.

Incubation period is the time between when a person is exposed to an illness and when they show symptoms.

Inoculated means to give a person exposure to a disease. Vaccines are used to inoculate people.

Long haulers are people who have not fully recovered from COVID-19 weeks or even months after first experiencing symptoms.

Mutations are changes that are random and by accident. Mutation is a normal process when viruses multiply and spread. These changes generally have little to no effect on a person's health. Sometimes, however, a mutation might cause a disease in a person.

Nucleic acid is the base unit of DNA and RNA, the substances that make up our genetic code.

Pathogen is any small organism that can cause disease, for example a virus or a bacterium.

Permissive refers to a permissive cell or host is one that allows a virus to get around its defenses and replicate.

Phospholipid membrane is a type of lipid that is an essential component of many biological membranes.

Post-acute COVID-19 syndrome is the lingering of symptoms in people who experience persistent COVID-19 symptoms weeks or even months after recovering from their initial illness.

Reassortment is when two or more different strains of a virus from different animal species combine in one intermediate host to form a new subtype strain, and the new strain spreads from the intermediate host to humans.

Spillover event is the term used to describe when a virus has overcome the many naturally occurring barriers necessary to "spill over" from one species to another.

Strain means a group of viruses that are genetically different from other groups of the same species.

Superspreader is someone who is highly contagious and spreads the virus to a large number of uninfected people.

Vaccines are substances that help the body create antibodies to fight a disease.

Vector is an organism, typically a biting insect or tick that transmits a disease or parasite from one animal or plant to another.

Wet market is an open place or covered building selling fresh meat, fish, and produce and dried goods like spices, flowers, and cooked meats. People who sell in a wet market ensure food is fresh, but there are high chances of contamination because it is an open market.

Zoonosis is an infection or disease that is transmissible from animals to humans under natural conditions. It is also an infection or disease that is transmissible between animals and humans.

References

Andersen, Kristian G., Andrew Rambaut, W. Ian Lipkin, Edward C. Holmes, and Robert F. Garry. "The Proximal Origin of SARS-CoV-2." Nature Medicine. Accessed November 29, 2020. *https://www.nature.com/articles/s41591-020-0820-9*

Bamford, D; Zucherman, M. "Encyclopedia of Virology", 4th ed, 2021, Elsevier Ltd ISBN 978-0-12-84515-9.

Calabrese, L.H. "Cytokine Storm and the Prospects for Immunotherapy with COVID-19." Cleve Clin J Med. Volume 87 Issue 7 (June 30, 2020):389-393. *https://doi.org/10.3949/ccjm.87a.ccc008*

Casanova, Lisa M., Soyoung Jeon, William A. Rutala, David J. Weber, and Mark D. Sobsey. "Effects of Air Temperature and Relative Humidity on Coronavirus Survival on Surfaces." Applied and Environmental Microbiology, Volume 76 Issue 9 (Apr 2010): 2712-2717. DOI: 10.1128/AEM.02291-09. *https://aem.asm.org/content/76/9/2712*

Cheng, Y.; Luo, R.; Wang, K.; Zhang, M.; Wang, Z.; Dong, L.; Li, J.; Yao, Y.; Ge, S.; Xu, G. "Kidney Impairment Is Associated with In-hospital Death of COVID-19 Patients.: Kidney International (2020) 97, 829–838; https://doi.org/10.1016/j.kint.2020.03.005

CDC. "COVID-19 and Animals." CDC website. Accessed November 29, 2020. *https://www.cdc.gov/coronavirus/2019-ncov/daily-life-coping/animals.htm*

CDC. "How the Flu Virus Can Change." CDC website. Accessed July 14, 2020. *https://www.cdc.gov/flu/about/viruses/change.htm*

CDC. "Scientific Brief: Community Use of Cloth Masks to Control the Spread of SARS-CoV-2." CDC website. Accessed December 14, 2020. *https://www.cdc.gov/coronavirus/2019-ncov/more/masking-science-sars-cov2.html*

Czeisler MÉ , Lane RI, Petrosky E, et al. Mental Health, Substance Use, and Suicidal Ideation During the COVID-19 Pandemic — United States, June 24–30, 2020. MMWR Morb Mortal Wkly Rep 2020; 69:1049–1057. DOI: *http://dx.doi.org/10.15585/mmwr.mm6932a1*

Fan, C., Lu, W., Kai, L., Ding, Y.and Wang, J. "ACE2 Expression in Kidney and Testis May Cause Kidney and Testis Damage After 2019-nCoV Infection." Frontiers in Medicine: January 2021 – Volume 7 – article 563893. *https://doi.org/10.3389/fmed.2020.563893*

Fehr, Anthony R., and Stanley Perlman. "Coronaviruses: An Overview of Their Replication and Pathogenesis." Coronaviruses. 2015; 1282: 1–23. *https://www.ncbi.nlm.nih.gov/pubmed/?term=Perlman%20S%5BAuthor%5D&cauthor=true&cauthor_uid=25720466*

Felsenstein, S., J.A. Herbert, P.S. McNamara, and C.M. Hedrich. "COVID-19: Immunology and Treatment Options." Clin Immunol. 2020 Jun; 215:108448. *https://doi.org/10.1016/j.clim.2020.108448*

Frutos, R., Serra-Cobo, J., Chen, T., & Devaux, C. A. (2020). "COVID-19: Time to exonerate the pangolin from the transmission of SARS-CoV-2 to humans." Infection, genetics and evolution: journal of molecular epidemiology and evolutionary genetics in infectious diseases, 84, 104493. *https://doi. org/10.1016/j.meegid.2020.104493*

Gaudreault, Natasha N., Jessie D. Trujillo, Mariano Carossino, David A. Meekins, Igor Morozov, Daniel W. Madden, Sabarish V. Indran, Dashzeveg Bold, Velmurugan Balaraman, Taeyong Kwon, Bianca Libanori Artiaga, Konner Cool, Adolfo García-Sastre, Wenjun Ma, William C. Wilson, Jamie Henningson, Udeni B. R. Balasuriya, and Juergen A. Richt. "SARS-CoV-2 Infection, Disease and Transmission in Domestic Cats." Emerging Microbes & Infections, 9:1, 2322-2332, DOI: 10.1080/22221751.2020.1833687

Guan, G.W., L. Gao, J.W. Wang, X.J. Wen, T.H. Mao, S.W. Peng, T. Zhang, X.M. Chen, and F.M. Lu. "Exploring the Mechanism of Liver Enzyme Abnormalities in Patients with Novel Coronavirus-infected Pneumonia." Chin. J. Hepatol. 2020, 28, E002.

Gunthe, S.S., Swain, B., Patra, S.S. et al. On the global trends and spread of the COVID-19 outbreak: preliminary assessment of the potential relation between location-specific temperature and UV index. J Public Health (Berl.) (2020). *https://doi.org/10.1007/s10389-020-01279-y*

Huang, C., Y. Wang, X. Li, L. Ren, J. Zhao, Y. Hu, L. Zhang, G. Fan, J. Xu, X. Gu, et al. "Clinical Features of Patients Infected with 2019 Novel Coronavirus in Wuhan, China." Lancet (Lond. Engl.) Volume 395 (2020): 497–506. *https://doi.org/10.1016/S0140-6736(20)30183-5*

Iravani, B., A. Arshamian, and A. Ravia, et al. "Relationship between Odor Intensity Estimates and COVID-19 Population Prediction in a Swedish Sample." Chem Senses. Volume 22 (May 2020): bjaa034. *https://doi.org/10.1101/2020.05.07.20094516; th*

Jin, Y., H. Yang, W. Ji, W. Wu, S. Chen, W. Zhang, and G. Duan. "Virology, Epidemiology, Pathogenesis, and Control of COVID-19." Viruses. Volume 12 issue 4 (Mar 27, 2020):372. *https://doi.org/10.3390/v12040372*

Kahn, Jeffrey S. MD, PhD*; McIntosh, Kenneth MD. "History and Recent Advances in Coronavirus Discovery." The Pediatric Infectious Disease Journal: November 2005 -Volume 24 - Issue 11 - p S223-S227 doi: 10.1097/01.inf.0000188166.17324.60 *https://journals.lww.com/pidj/Fulltext/2005/11001/History_and_ Recent_Advances_in_Coronavirus.12.aspx*

Kampf, G. "Efficacy of Ethanol against Viruses in Hand Disinfection." J Hosp Infect. Volume 98, issue 4 (Apr 2018):331-338. *https://doi.org/10.1016/j.jhin.2017.08.025*

Lee, S., T. Kim, and E. Lee, et al. "Clinical Course and Molecular Viral Shedding Among Asymptomatic and Symptomatic Patients with SARS-CoV-2 Infection in a Community Treatment Center in the Republic of Korea." JAMA Intern Med. Volume 180 issue 11 (2020):1447–1452. doi:10.1001/jamainternmed.2020.3862

Letzer, Rafi. "The Coronavirus Didn't Really Start at that Wuhan 'Wet Market.'" LiveScience.Accessed November 29, 2020. *https://www. livescience.com/covid-19-did-not-start-at-wuhanwet-market.html*

Malone, J., Del Rosario Perez, M., Friberg, E. G., Prokop, M., Jung, S. E., Griebel, J., & Ebdon-Jackson, S. (2016). Justification of CT for Individual Health Assessment of Asymptomatic Persons: A World Health Organization Consultation. Journal of the American College of Radiology : JACR, 13(12 Pt A), 1447–1457.e1. *https://doi.org/10.1016/j.jacr.2016.07.020*

McIntosh K. (1974) Coronaviruses: A Comparative Review. In: Arber W. et al. (eds) Current Topics in Microbiology and Immunology / Ergebnisse der Mikrobiologie und Immunitätsforschung. Current Topics in Microbiology and Immunology / Ergebnisse der Mikrobiologie und Immunitätsforschung, vol 63. Springer, Berlin, Heidelberg. *https://doi.org/10.1007/978-3-642-65775-7_3*

Mousavizadeh, L., and S. Ghasemi. "Genotype and Phenotype of COVID-19: Their Roles in Pathogenesis." J Microbiol Immunol Infect. (Mar 31, 2020). *https://doi.org/10.1016/j.jmii.2020.03.022*

Ng, W. M., Stelfox, A. J., & Bowden, T. A. (2020). Unraveling virus relationships by structure-based phylogenetic classification. Virus evolution, 6(1), veaa003. *https://doi.org/10.1093/ve/veaa003*

Nuwer, R. "Why the world needs viruses to function". BBC Future,17th June 2020 *https://www.bbc.com/future/article/20200617-what-if-all-viruses-disappeared.*

Nieman Foundation. "Covering Pandemic Flu." Nieman Foundation for Journalism at Harvard. Accessed: August 23, 2020. *https://nieman. harvard.edu/wp-content/uploads/podassets/microsites/ NiemanGuideToCoveringPandemicFlu/TheScience/ HowFluVirusesChange.aspx.html*

Oran, D.P., and E.J. "Topol. Prevalence of Asymptomatic SARS-CoV-2 Infection : A Narrative Review." Ann Intern Med. Volume 173, issue 5 (September 1, 2020):362-367. *doi:10.3949/ccjm.87a.ccc008*

Racaniello, Vincent. "Simplifying Virus Classification: The Baltimore System." Virology Blog. Accessed July 6, 2020. *https://www.virology. ws/2009/08/12/simplifying-virus-classification-thebaltimore-system/*

Rothe, C., M. Schunk, and P. Sothmann, et al. "Transmission of 2019-nCoV Infection from an Asymptomatic Contact in Germany." The New England Journal of Medicine. Volume 382, issue 10 (2020):970-971. DOI: 10.1056/NEJMc2001468

Sinclair, R.M.; Ravantti, J.J. and Bamford, D. "Nucleic and Amino Acid Sequences Support Structure-Based Viral Classification". Journal of Virology: April 2017 – Volume 91 – Issue 8 – e02275-16. *https://doi. org/10.1128/JVI.02275-16*

The WHO Rapid Evidence Appraisal for COVID-19 Therapies (REACT) Working Group. Association Between Administration of Systemic Corticosteroids and Mortality Among Critically Ill Patients With COVID-19: A Meta-analysis. JAMA. 2020;324(13):1330–1341.doi:10.1001/ jama.2020.17023

University of Glasgow. "Researchers Identify Evolutionary Origins of SARS-CoV-2." Phys.org. Accessed November 29, 2020. *https://phys. org/news/2020-07-evolutionary-sars-cov-.html*

Wei, W.E. L.Z., C.J. Chiew, S.E. Yong, M.P. Toh, and V.J.Lee. "Presymptomatic Transmission of SARS-CoV-2 — Singapore, January 23–March 16, 2020." MMWR Morbidity and Mortality Weekly Report. ePub (April 1, 2020). *https://www.cdc.gov/mmwr/volumes/69/wr/pdfs/mm6914e1-H.pdf*

World Health Organization. "Naming the Coronavirus Disease (COVID-19) and the Virus that Causes It." World Health Organization website. Accessed July 1, 2020. *https://www.who.int/emergencies/ diseases/novel-coronavirus-2019/technical-guidance/naming-the-coronavirus-disease-(covid-2019)-and-the-virus-that-causes-it*

World Health Organization. "Origins of SARS-CoV-2." World Health Organization website. Accessed November 29, 2020. *https://apps.who. int/iris/bitstream/handle/10665/332197/WHO-2019-nCoV-FAQ-Virus_origin-2020.1-eng.pdf?sequence=1&isAllowed=y*

Wu, X., Nethery, R. C., Sabath, B. M., Braun, D., & Dominici, F. (2020). Exposure to air pollution and COVID-19 mortality in the United States: A nationwide cross-sectional study. medRxiv : the preprint server for health sciences, 2020.04.05.20054502. *https://doi. org/10.1101/2020.04.05.20054502*

Xiao, F.; Tang, M.; Zheng, X.; Li, C.; He, J.; Hong, Z.; Huang, S.; Zhang, Z.; Lin, X.; Fang, Z.; et al. "Evidence for gastrointestinal infection of SARS-CoV-2." J. Gastroenterology: May 2020 – Volume 158 – Issue 6 – p. 1831 –1833. *https://doi.org/10.1053/j.gastro.2020.02.055*

Yu Chen, Qianyun Liu, and Deyin Guo. "Emerging coronaviruses: Genome structure, replication, and pathogenesis" J Med Virol: April 2020 - Volume 92 - Issue 4 – p. 418–423. *https://doi.org/10.1002/jmv.25681*

Useful Links

World Health Organization

https://www.who.int/emergencies/diseases/novel-coronavirus-2019

Centers for Disease Control and Prevention

https://www.cdc.gov/coronavirus/2019-ncov/

For my parents, Jean Persad and Ramsaran Ramnanan

This book is dedicated to our medical professionals
and other responders who step out tirelessly
and unselfishly to care for and save the lives of others.
We are grateful for your tireless work.
We thank you. We salute you.

The text and schematics aim to explain concepts of biology
and are simplified to aid understanding. The information presented here are
for informational and educational purposes only and does not constitute any
health or medical advice. Please seek advice from your healthcare provider
or doctor for your particular health concerns before changing your
healthcare routine or relying on this information.

Virology editor Camilly P. Pires de Mello, PhD
Virology editor Viveca Giongo, PhD

Editor Alana Joli Abbott
Editor Vicky Garrard
Proofreader Isabella Piestrzynska
Art director/book design Lynne Moulding
Publishing manager Sabbithry Persad

Library of Congress Control Number: 2021913597

First paperback edition August 2021

Publisher's Cataloging-In-Publication Data
(Prepared by The Donohue Group, Inc.)

Names: Persad, Sabbithry, author. | Mello, Camilly P. Pires de, editor. | Giongo, Viveca, editor.
Title: What is coronavirus? : how it infects, how it spreads, and how to stay safe /
written by Sabbithry Persad, MBA ; edited by Camilly P. Pires de Mello, PhD [and] Viveca
Giongo, PhD. Description: First paperback edition. | Orlando, FL : Firewater Media Group, 2021. |
Interest age level: 12 and up. | Includes bibliographical references. | Summary: "The coronavirus
pandemic can be scary and hard to understand for both young readers and adults!
This book explains the SARS-CoV-2 virus, the diseases it causes, and the steps
to keep people safe and curb the spread. Readers also learn about past
pandemics and how they ended …"--Provided by publisher.
Identifiers: ISBN 9780981243931
Subjects: LCSH: COVID-19 (Disease)--Juvenile literature. | Coronaviruses--Juvenile literature. |
Epidemics--Juvenile literature. | CYAC: COVID-19 (Disease) | Coronaviruses. | Epidemics.
Classification: LCC RA644.C67 P47 2021 | DDC 614.592414--dc23

ISBN 978-0-9812439-3-1 (pbk.)

Printed in U.S. and Canada.

1 3 5 7 9 10 8 6 4 2

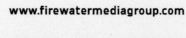

www.firewatermediagroup.com